THE ANATOMY OF ILLUSION

MICHAEL ENGLISH / THE ANATOMY OF ILLUSION
A PAINTER'S GUIDE TO HYPER-REALIST TECHNIQUE

TO JACQUELINE, MY DEAREST WIFE

An imprint of Dragon's World Limited

Dragon's World Limited
Limpsfield
Surrey RH8 0DY
Great Britain

First published by Dragon's World 1989
© Dragon's World 1989
© Michael English 1989

British Library Cataloguing in Publication Data

English, Michael
   Anatomy of illusion: a painter's guide
   to hyper-realist technique
   1. Painting. Techniques
   I. Title
   751.4

ISBN Hardback 1 85028 079 7
      Limpback 1 85028 080 0

Typeset by Bookworm Typesetting, Manchester, England

Printed in Singapore

PREFACE

It has always struck me that, while critics talk about style and content in works of art, artists tend to pass these by and talk obsessively about technique. For the artist everything is in the *how* — how to find the best method of realising the idea. The idea itself he takes for granted. Michael English's book is a fascinating example of this syndrome. There is, however, much more to it than that. 'How to' books of the normal kind are usually impersonal. Do this, do that, then do the other — and you will achieve the result you want. This book, by contrast, has an emotional commitment to what is being described which makes the text moving as well as fascinating.

This effect is the more surprising because the basic technique discussed — the use of the airbrush — is often condemned for its lack of true personality. Airbrushed work does not, it is said, exhibit any kind of thumbprint. There is no real physical connection between the artist and what he is making and the results thus fall below the level of true art. English demonstrates that all this is mere propaganda. The truly creative artist chooses the method which best suits his purpose. In English's case, this purpose is to produce a simulacrum of reality whose effect is more intense than that produced by any photograph. His paintings, in fact, offer a way of seeing which is more penetrating than anything the camera can manage.

Of course, since I am a critic, not an artist, I have to ask myself *why* as well as *how*. There is in western art a long tradition of hyper-realistic representation. In fact, this is one of the things which most strikingly differentiates the western tradition from others. The Roman author Pliny tells a story about an Ancient Greek artist who painted grapes which were so realistic that even the birds were deceived, and came to peck at them. One could perhaps argue that our admiration for work of this type springs from naive astonishment at mere dexterity: and this admiration inevitably diminishes after the deception is exposed (the birds Pliny mentions no doubt flew away disappointed). My own belief is that one ought to take hyper-realism very seriously. Representational art serves many purposes. One is to connect inner and outer — our subjective feelings about the world, and its intractable otherness.

The kind of art Michael English makes breaks down the barrier between the two — or almost breaks it. It asserts that it is possible to bring at least a small fragment of external reality into complete harmony with what is within us: the artist has done so, therefore the spectator can do so too. Yet of course, as English reminds us in this book, it never quite works. The artistic tension lies in the fact that there is still a gap. The narrower it becomes, the more electric the charge generated.

There is something else as well. I have already used the word "fragment". Something else which Michael English points out is the fact that the hyper-realistic image is always, and inevitably, a part not a whole, a piece wrenched almost at random from a larger continuum. What he might have added is that this piece, this fragment, when removed from the actual presence of what it imitates, acquires an integrity, and thus a kind of intransigence of its own. When we look at a hyper-realist painting some of its effect comes from its apparently seamless unity with what the artist has actually seen, and some from its often violent discontinuity with its actual surroundings. We witness an argument between the "reality" embodied in the painting, and (to coin a tautology) the real reality of its context. Once again there is a gap — and once again that gap is the essential stimulant to both perception and imagination.

EDWARD LUCIE-SMITH

CONTENTS

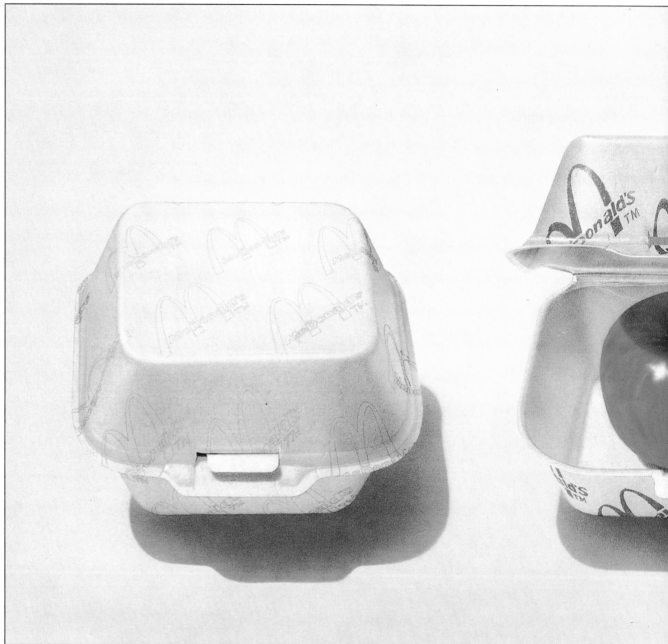

Untitled 1986

Lithograph commissioned by Leo
Burnett Inc. to celebrate their
acquisition of the McDonalds account.

INTRODUCTION

Though this book concerns itself primarily with the explanation of the techniques I have employed in all my works, it also shows, through this exposure, the forces that have driven me to the position that I now find myself in. A painter whose art is an art of imitation.

But that is a simple explanation of a motive that is very complicated indeed. Because in my obsessional desire to imitate the world that I find outside myself, I create a new object. A painting that stands in the world by itself, though it be merely a representation of something else.

My concern with detail and accuracy has grown from a desire to experience the most intimate secrets of that which I have found. Even my early prints of processed food products were attempts to achieve truthful accuracy. They failed, of course, but in their failure created something new.

Now I am closer to that truthful imitation, and I have arrived here by technique. But can it be said that the closer I come to that truth the more sterile my work becomes? When the personality of the object dominates my own personality, is it then a mere photograph? A dull snapshot from a discarded photograph album? I don't know. I really don't know.

But I must pursue this quarry. Though it is leading me further and further away from the mainstream of contemporary art, I cannot turn back. The beauty of the world outside myself interests me more than the one within. And the beauty of the mastery of a craft holds me far more than freedom of self-expression and all the loose laid-back attitudes that go with it.

My paintings are precision imitations of microcosms of reality. They are, I hope, the work of a craftsman.

The success of Hyper Realism relies on its ability to activate learned responses. There is a threshold you must pass in order to provoke these responses; this is the secret of the mystery of illusion. It is nothing to do with photography, which is a recording medium. Its task is re-creation, or at least the illusion of re-creation.

Our learned responses are the fruits of all our experiences from the moment of our birth, and perhaps before. What we see is not

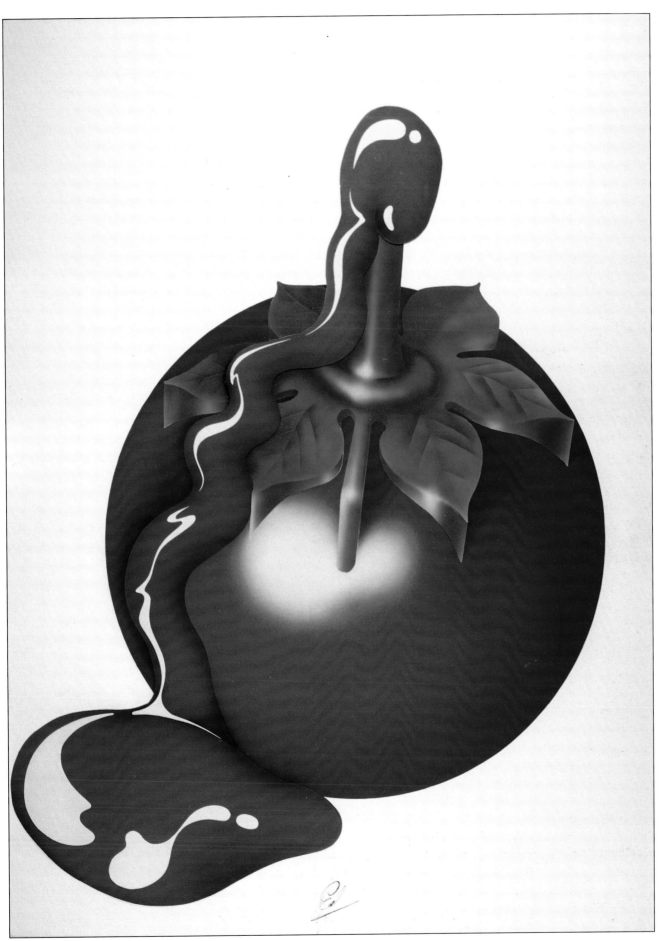

Ketchup 1969

reality, but a learned attitude towards reality. When we are confronted by a McDonald's milk shake, we know it is a Mac milk shake because that is what we have learned a milk shake looks like. We respond accordingly.

Now my particular brand of Hyper Realism seeks to outsmart this process. When you activate a response synthetically, the result is confusion. The observer has to cope with two responses; one, the milk shake, and two, the paint. It is this confusion that is the thrill of Hyper Realism. This is further complicated by the injection of my own personality – the fire to cook the soup.

In this respect I am actually playing with the process of our observation of the world. Sometimes successfully, but more often unsuccessfully. In this game I have sought to clarify in my own mind the process of observation, the relationship between my thought and the world outside my thought. The relationship between what is real and what is illusion; what I see and what I think I see.

Though I was not consciously aware of it at the time, this interest was especially active in the early '70s with the 'Nature' pictures. These paintings have been criticized as being badly constructed – even called 'not real paintings'. But this was exactly the point. They are badly constructed – purposefully. As though an incident or object had caught my eye and a frame was thrown down around it. The frame would never encompass a brilliant composition, only a piece of a greater composition that is never shown.

It was my discovery of the airbrush in 1968, the result of a chance remark by a Royal College of Art student, that made this journey of discovery possible. For the airbrush, with its ability to imitate the fine gradations of light on objects, opened a door into a garden of colour and form that I never knew existed. But as we shall see in later chapters that door is not an easy one to unlock.

With the coming of the Seventies I was set for a new style, a new look, and a new energy. I was aware, concurrent with my own work, of a new art movement in the United States, Hyper Realism. I was amazed how the theories of this art coincided so closely with my own. I thought I was alone in the quest to achieve an art that transcended the human touch. I wasn't, and this knowledge drove

Angel Delight 1975

me on from the now famous series of prints into real paintings on real canvas. And real was the word. Because, where you can see my failure to transcend the man-made look in my prints, the paintings, both the Nature series and the subsequent Machine series, really reached out to that goal of ultimate illusion. It took ten years to crack it.

Though just as painstaking as that of the American realists, my work was more concerned with imitating the object. I have always attempted to convey the feel and smell of the objects. To cross the boundaries of the senses, to evoke, by sheer painting alone, the sense of smell, sound and touch. In my early work the by-product of this technique has been a certain sexuality, which receded as I became more intensely involved with the mechanics of imagery rather than the mechanics of communication. Even in the painting *Ozonothérapie Combinée*, into which it is possible to read all sorts of sexual and cultural connotations, my chief concern was with the image, the construction of the machine, and the composition. It was taken from a tiny photograph in a brochure for steam baths. The result surprised me, as did the look on the model's face! Was she a modern Mona Lisa? Now all smooth and crisp, naked inside warm plastic.

I believe that without the airbrush the whole art movement of Photo Realism, Hyper Realism, New Wave Realism, Super Realism, or whatever of the 1970's, could never have happened. The unique ability of the airbrush to imitate the properties of light made possible the illusions that are so characteristic of that movement. There have been many books on the technique of airbrushing, but none have shown what it feels like to use one. The thrill of completely mastering it so as to become at one with it. Like pointing your finger at the canvas and seeing the colour and form appear. I never forget the excitement and satisfaction I felt when I peeled off the mask on the *Coke Cap* painting and saw that the liquid was really real. That was something I could not have achieved with the paintbrush. For the paintbrush lets in the human touch; it makes something look man-made. Not fallen from the sky.

The food and rubbish paintings of 1969 and 1970 were not my first airbrush work. There had been at least a year of hard work and

Mouthmill, North Devon 1980

This painting marked the climax of all my
nature work in the 1970's. It has no equal.

Ozonothérapie Combineé 1979

disappointment before then, of repeated attempts to find the key.
The airbrush was not easy to master. I had no one to teach me, no
guide books, I made many mistakes. I used anything. I made copies
of George Petty pin-up girls. I put a 74-page comic book together, a
disastrous operation. I produced some awful posters in my old
psychedelic style, but airbrushed.

It was after a chance remark from the poet Christopher Logue
that I found that key. After looking at a very early silk-screened
poster of a pair of lips, he suggested I shove an ice cream into
them. Those Tom Wesselman-inspired lips turned out to be the way
forward. Throughout my psychedelic period there was always a
strain of pop art just below the surface. Now it could come out in full
force — as the Food series.

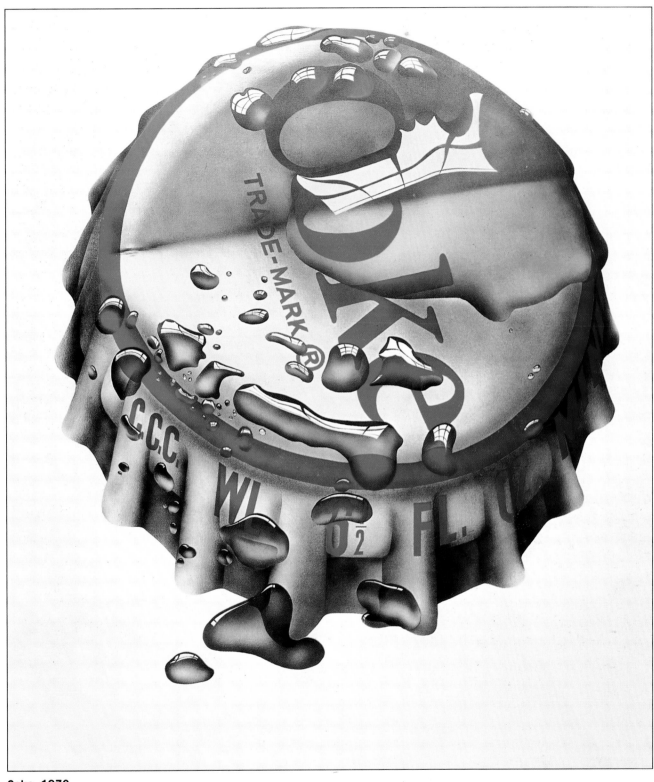

Coke 1970

In many ways this adoption of the airbrush was a quite natural development of the silk-screening I had been doing in the Sixties, both on T-shirts in '65 and posters in '67. Both processes use a masking system, the silk screen with its photosensitive film and the airbrush with its adhesive film. The difference was, of course, in the detail that the latter could handle. I still love the silk screen to this day and look for another chance to use its beautiful tactile qualities.

Perhaps the best known of all my early Realist work, this has become a cliché of the Super-Realist style. Painted on canvas, the original represents the first tentative steps into distortion.

Message 2 1968   A poster created in collaboration with Allen Ginsberg.

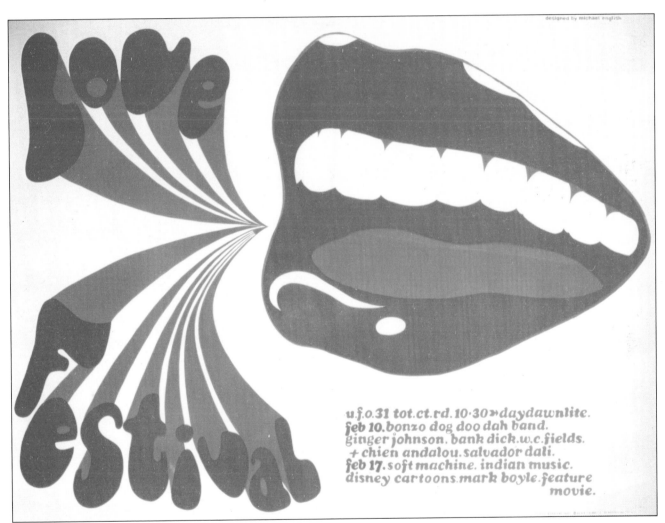

designed by michael english

u.f.o.31 tot.ct.rd.10·30×daydawnlite.
feb 10.bonzo dog doo dah band.
ginger johnson. bank dick.w.c.fields.
+ chien andalou. salvador dali.
feb 17.soft machine. indian music.
disney cartoons.mark boyle.feature
                                    movie.

Love Festival   1967
One of the first of my 1960's posters.
It should be called 'Homage to Tom
Wesselman'!

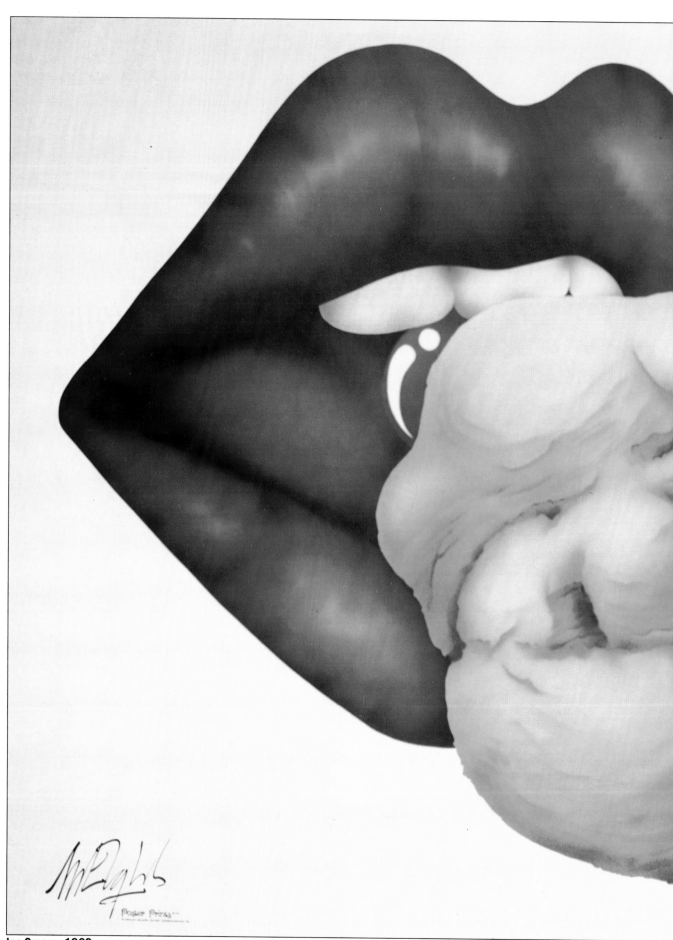

Ice Cream 1969

This print was my second attempt at an ice cream. The first one — it was vanilla flavoured — was given to Christopher Logue the poet, who tells me it was lost somewhere in Spain.

INTRODUCTION

Syrup drawing

Bisto Kids 1971   A portrait of John and Jean Gilbert.

Yellow 1978

A silk-screen print with dirt and grime finished by hand. The dirt was applied semi-randomly; each print is unique, as each locomotive is rendered unique by time and weather.

A poster project for the singer and actress Toyah. In order to save money, sheets of newspaper were used instead of clear paper; the image was then to be silk-screened on top. A good example of how the artist can capitalize on limitation.

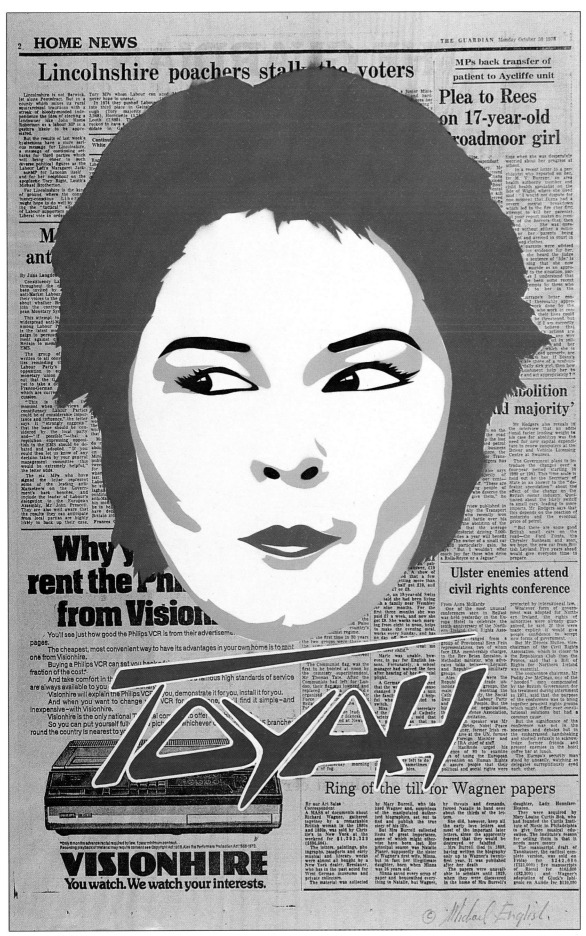

Toyah 1979

A steam trawler

BEGINNINGS

Drawing and painting have always been the most important part of my life. A means of capturing and holding an experience, of making it last longer. I want to take you back as far as I can remember, back to the years when the deepest influences were being formed, when I became conscious of the world about me and drawing became a way of expressing that consciousness.

When I was 5 and 6, in the late 1940's, we lived in a bungalow in Crail in Scotland. The little house looked out over the sand and across the Firth of Forth to May Island. On grey wild days you would see me in the bay window, with a pencil and sheet of paper torn from the back of a book, staring out to sea, trying to get down on that paper the drama before me. The black shapes of steam trawlers working out of Anstruther, their tanned mizzen sails spread triangular behind a tall smoke stack, black smoke streams out ahead, the ships alternately appearing and disappearing as they plunged into the grey sea, spray boiling over the foredeck. I made countless attempts to capture that vision. I never got it.

Can you imagine my feelings one day when I encountered one close at hand? We passed her on a sailing trip out to May Island. She looked magnificent, her long body sliding strongly through the water. I could see all the detail, all the colour. The black hull, the red and black funnel, the stitching on the sail, everything.

Since those years, as I moved into different environments, my passions changed from fishing boats to the railways, from the railways to aircraft, and back again.

When my father, an RAF officer, was posted down to Hitchin in Hertfordshire, I would spend almost every day of my school holidays down at Hitchin station. I can still see today the spot where I sat, a solitary little figure, watching the King's Cross expresses fly by, invariably hauled by those magnificent Gresley A-4 Pacifics. This was the 1950's and steam ruled on British Railways. The hours I spent enduring the boredom of passing local trains with B-1s or V-2's at their head, or the blackened War Department 2-8-0's with their long dirty coal trains, just to catch that fleeting glimpse of those streamlined greyhounds of the North Eastern. And, at night, as I lay in bed, I could hear the lonesome howl of their whistles as they sped northwards with the night expresses.

An A-4 Pacific locomotive

These images and sounds sank deep inside me, and lay hidden
until many years later. At the time, though, I was unable to put them
into any coherent form. I had very little grasp of composition and
was quite unable to comprehend perspective. Still, I knew they
existed as pictures, and I wrestled with them. But always alone.
There was no one to help me. This solitary struggle for self-
expression that was so characteristic of my youth stays with me to
this day. It is an unfortunate trait of my character that has so often
alienated me from the mainstream of art. I became too self-reliant
too soon. It has brought me a lot of unhappiness. The few times I
was fortunate enough to be part of a group of friends and
associates, at art school and during the late 1960's, I discovered I
had a limitless capacity for enjoyment and I actually became more
productive and a lot more likeable.

The first real decision I ever made was at the age of 21, in 1962.
I had control of my life and I was going to Art School. I *had* to learn
to draw. I left home and came to London. Finding a little room in
Oxford Road, Chiswick, I applied to St Martin's School of Art. They
were full up that year but the Principal was very excited and
telephoned Hammersmith School of Art. I was accepted on the spot.
There really were some people who liked what I was doing! I stayed
a year but was unable to crack any of the problems that had beset
me previously. I really was depressed. I just couldn't get what I
wanted on to paper. The times I went into life-drawing class
determined to do a masterpiece were countless. I could not
translate the three-dimensional into the two-dimensional. I just
couldn't do it. And having to work in a coffee-bar until 12 o'clock
every night didn't help either.

But something was about to happen that would change everything and release all that energy I had locked up for so many years.
Because I lived in Chiswick, in order to receive a grant, I had to
leave Hammersmith School of Art and go to Ealing, a move which
coincided with the first experiment in a new approach to art
teaching — the Ground Course. I felt re-born. I felt as though
everything I touched turned to gold. Midas. I read Paul Klee's
Thinking Eye, I read Bertrand Russell, Wittgenstein, E.H. Gombrich.
I discovered the meaning of abstraction and realism. that a line or a

No. 75027 1976

Painting this was re-living a lost
childhood. Before I could really launch
myself into machine realism, I had to
lay this ghost from the past.

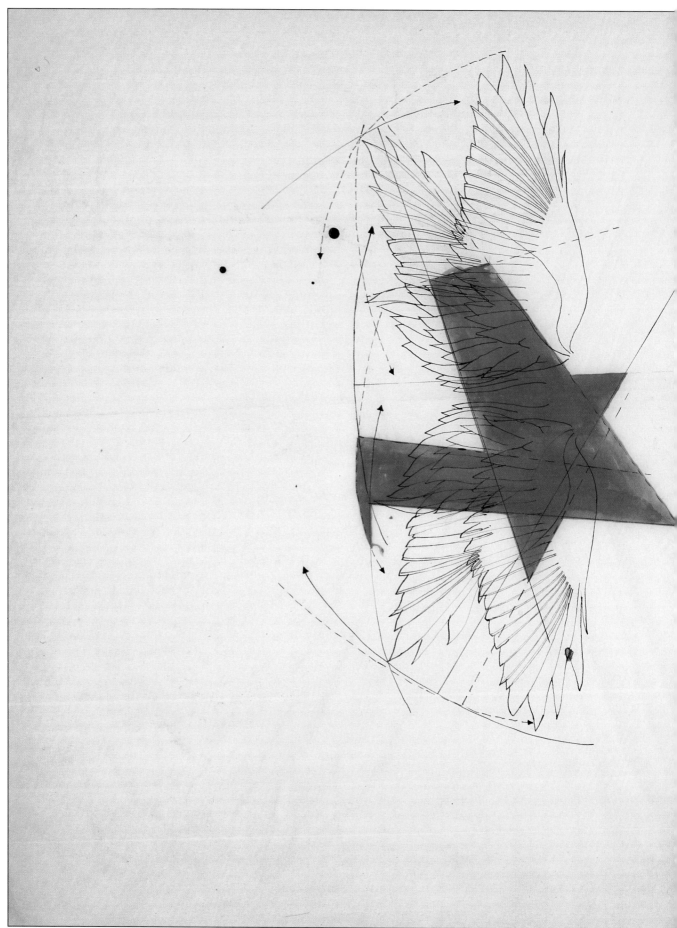

Flight Geometry 1963

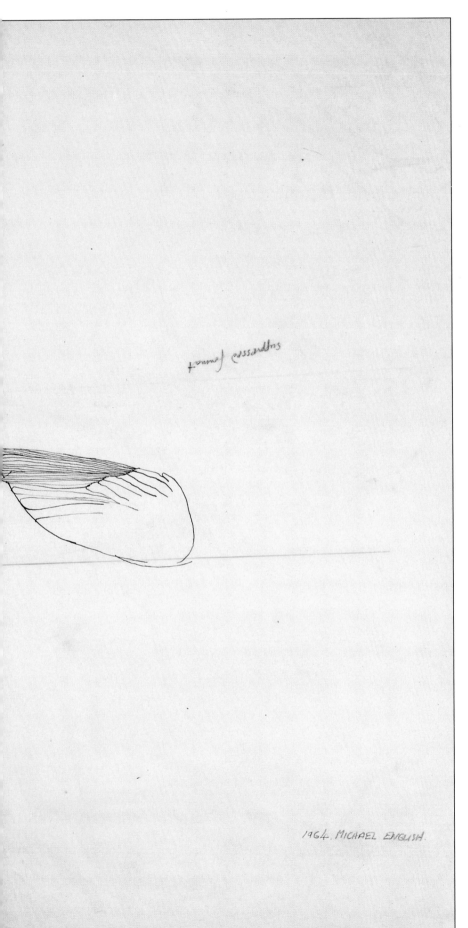

1964. MICHAEL ENGLISH.

The earliest piece of work I have. Done when I was a student, it shows the love of analysis I had even then.

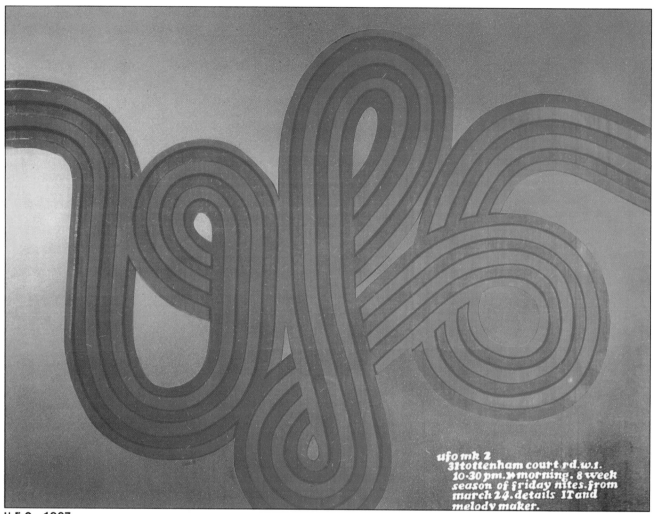

U.F.O. 1967

mark is an individual in itself. I read C.G. Jung's *Archetypes and the Collective Subconscious,* and discussed Symbolism and the interpretation of dreams and how Art is closely allied to many forms of neurosis. The Artist and the Madman were brothers. All this was a long way from drawing fishing boats, but this was what it was all about. This is what I wanted.

It came as a shock to me that after being the star pupil of the Ealing School of Art, I should have an application to the Royal College of Art rejected. After three years of everybody saying yes, the big No hit me hard. But I carried on undaunted. Things would be a lot more difficult now. I would miss the contacts and help such an influential academy could offer. But I was armed with an ability and a talent that I trusted would see me through.

I drifted away from the world of painting and, in association with the shop 'Gear' in Carnaby Street, gravitated towards Design. Primarily for finance but also because I enjoyed the direct communication with a new audience. Young, swinging England! I used the silk screen for the first time and revelled in the bright clear colours and the fabulous tactile quality of the ink. Carrier bags, sun glasses and T-shirts were my speciality. Everyone was wearing them, everyone was carrying them. John Lennon was refused entry into Greece because he was wearing a JESUS SAVES T-shirt. You couldn't move in my little flat for carrier bags and T-shirts. I had a

I believe this is the best poster I have ever done. Silk-screen printed in Dayglo on gold ink, the message integrates with the image in a strong, clean way. These posters were displayed in multiples, on walls, buildings sites and derelict shops. The effect was stunning.

Shopfront on Chelsea Green, London 1966

mail order deal with *Honey* magazine that I could never hope to complete.

It all got too much and I wasn't earning much money so I gave it up. Then in the summer of '66 when they were shooting *Blow-Up* outside my brightly painted front door, Michael Rainey knocked and came in. And for me that was the end of the old world and the beginning of the new world of love, peace and LSD. Turn on, Tune in, Drop out. I was already well out and tuned in, so it wasn't too difficult. There followed the shop-front design of Hung on You, a very Roy Liechtenstein affair, and a partnership with Nigel Waymouth that was to really blossom into that riot of colour and art nouveau pastiche — the psychedelic poster. We turned out so many. All the groups wanted a poster.

This, together with Nigel´s natural charm, was to become a passport into all the fashionable groups of the time. You would see us one night sharing a table with the Beatles, another going into the Fulham Road Tandoori with Brian Jones. No. 100 Cheyne Walk, the home of Christopher Gibbs, was a popular venue and I spent many enjoyable evenings there. There was really no end to it. I knew Brian during the latter years of his life. His asthma, coupled with a dependence on vodka and LSD, caused little concern. No one at the time realized the dangers of drug taking; no one could foresee the casualties that were to follow.

And of course, the more fashionable we were the more in demand were our posters. We signed a contract with a publisher and began selling them. This was the beginning of the poster business that was to boom well into the late ´70´s.

Surprisingly, though, we were entirely cut off from the current Art Scene in London. Try as I may the doors were kept firmly closed. They weren´t going to allow the hippies into their ordered world of Art Finance. They kept with their Richard Hamiltons, their Paolozzis and their David Hockneys, who were, I admit, painting real paintings rather than posting posters. And my current passport did say designer and not artist. I wasn´t satisfied.

It was after a trip to Amsterdam where we performed as a musical group Hapshash and the Coloured Coat, a name we borrowed from our poster design business, that I decided to break from the whole psychedelic/hippy scene and go out alone to search for something new and, for me at that time, more fruitful. Thus entered the airbrush and the consequent struggle to master it and turn it into a powerful and creative instrument.

Porsche advertisement

An advertisement for Porsche cars. I owe a great debt to the advertising industry. Without its help and financial support I could never have survived as an artist. The galleries and museums would have frozen me out.

Flight 704 1979

The groundwork for this painting was indirectly financed by the Coca-Cola Company, who paid for a return flight to New York – the midday TWA flight 704. The huge Boeing 747 wing sweeps majestically out to the horizon. We sit in a limbo of eternal sunshine listening to the hiss of the freezing air rushing over the fuselage. Free of the burden of life.

EQUIPMENT & APPLICATIONS

The airbrush is just one of a group of machines and instruments that rely on a common principle, one of the laws of fluidics. When a fluid or gas is drawn at high speed over a nozzle, it creates a low-pressure vortex at the tip of that nozzle. This low pressure will draw anything into it, be it paint, water, sand or powder. Once in the low-pressure area, the fluid is sucked into the high-speed air stream, where it diffuses with the air molecules — atomizes — to form a fine spray. The higher the speed of the air stream, the greater the vacuum and thus the greater the volume of liquid it will draw, within the limitation of nozzle size. Of course, the high-speed stream need not necessarily be air, it can be any fluid. The injectors of a steam locomotive, for instance, use steam under pressure to draw water into the boiler without having to lower the pressure of that boiler. The carburettor in a motor car uses the passage of air at high speed to draw petrol from a nozzle, called a jet, into its cylinders for combustion.

A 'double action' airbrush (the most popular type) has two valves which allow control of the spray. The air volume — and consequently speed, since it is all going through the same narrow passage — is controlled by a ball-and-seat valve immediately below the lever; the paint volume by a needle which seats in the tapered nozzle just inside the outer tip. On a gravity-fed double action airbrush such as the DeVilbiss Super 63, these two valves are linked so you can actually tune the *ratio* of paint to air as well as their speed and volume. 'Spray pattern', or spread of paint, is altered slightly as you increase the paint flow, but accurate adjustment of the pattern more properly depends on a nozzle which moves in relation to the outer tip. Spray guns allow adjustment, airbrushes on the whole don't.

Both the airbrush and the spray gun use compressed air as the propellant. This is supplied by a compressor, but you can buy disposable cans of compressed air rather like aerosol cans but without the spray nozzle. Aerosols do not use compressed air but compressed Chloro-fluoro carbon Gas (C.F.C.) which does not react with paints or other chemicals. (I don't use aerosols, chiefly because of the poisonous nature of the paints, but also because I prefer to avoid contributing to the destruction of our planet's ozone layer. There's enough damage been done already!)

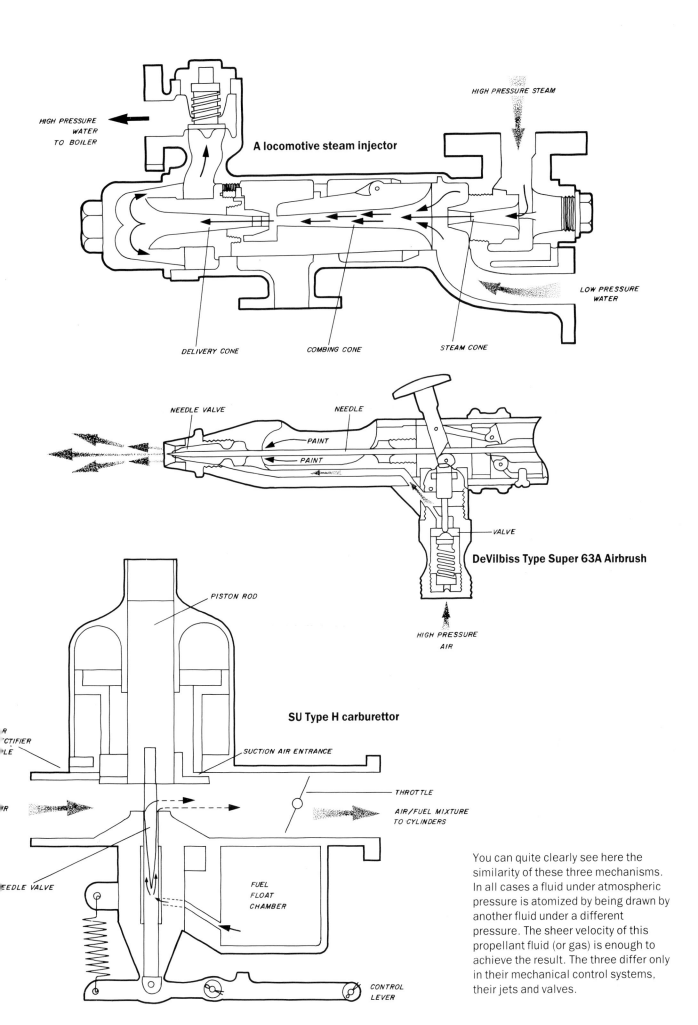

HIGH PRESSURE STEAM

HIGH PRESSURE
WATER
TO BOILER

A locomotive steam injector

LOW PRESSURE
WATER

DELIVERY CONE COMBING CONE STEAM CONE

NEEDLE VALVE NEEDLE

PAINT

PAINT

VALVE

DeVilbiss Type Super 63A Airbrush

HIGH PRESSURE
AIR

PISTON ROD

R
CTIFIER
LE

SUCTION AIR ENTRANCE

SU Type H carburettor

THROTTLE

R AIR/FUEL MIXTURE
TO CYLINDERS

FUEL
FLOAT
CHAMBER

EEDLE VALVE

CONTROL
LEVER

You can quite clearly see here the similarity of these three mechanisms. In all cases a fluid under atmospheric pressure is atomized by being drawn by another fluid under a different pressure. The sheer velocity of this propellant fluid (or gas) is enough to achieve the result. The three differ only in their mechanical control systems, their jets and valves.

Compressor

It's important to remember that all sprayed paint, water colour or cellulose, is dangerous. You must wear a really good high-quality mask when working large areas. In the old days of the Rubbish series prints I would emerge from the studio with a ring of green or red paint around my nose. I sneezed pink and coughed indigo. You have been warned!

Compressor

The compressor I have always used (I bought it in 1968) is a DeVilbiss continuous pressure machine. It has an air reservoir tank connected to a compressor, which is controlled automatically by a pressure-sensitive switch. When the pressure drops below 30psi, the motor cuts in and pumps air into the tank until it reaches the required pressure, in my case 40psi. So I always have pressure on hand, and I don't have to put up with the continuous rattle of a straight-through type. But it does have one drawback; it takes time for the motor to pump up to the pressure I need, and especially when I'm using the larger DeVilbiss MP gun, which really throws the paint out, I have to stand there champing at the bit, waiting for the needle to get back to 40 or 45psi. I hate hanging about. Still, we've put up with each other all these years so I can't be that dissatisfied.

X Marks the Spot 1986
Commissioned by a Swiss collector.
This work shows a sophistication of
observation unknown to my old style, in
which it was purposely conceived.

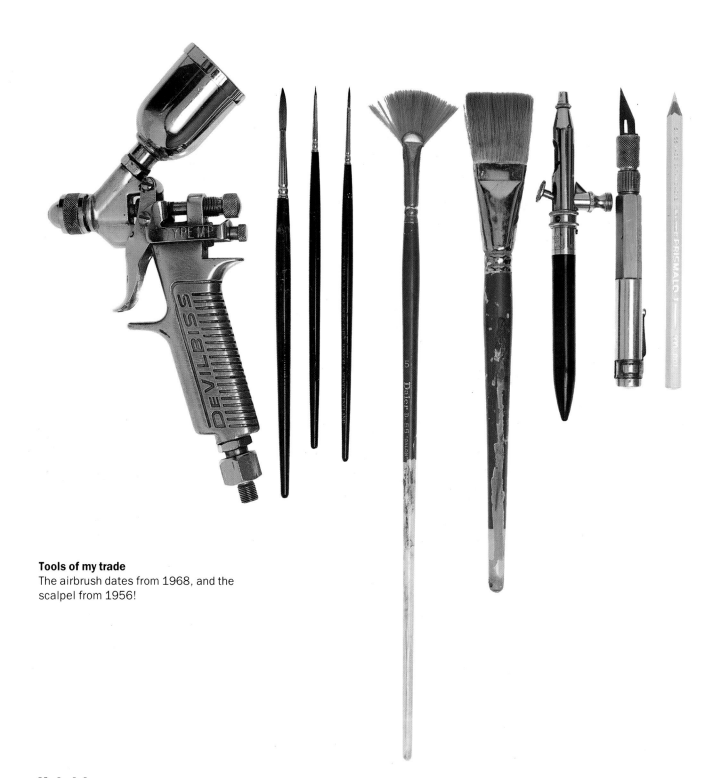

Tools of my trade
The airbrush dates from 1968, and the scalpel from 1956!

Hairdrier

The hairdrier is another indispensable tool in my work. It speeds up the drying time of paint, freeing me from the interminable waiting between coats. But remember that a hairdrier can get very hot, so it must not be held less than half a metre from the canvas. Anything nearer and you will boil the paint and melt the mask, a catastrophe in any language. Just play the warm air gently over the surface and be patient. It's still a whole lot quicker than no hairdrier at all.

I don't recommend using a hairdrier on oil-based paints unless the colour layer is very thin. Warming the paint only softens it. These paints cannot be hurried, they must be left to dry naturally.

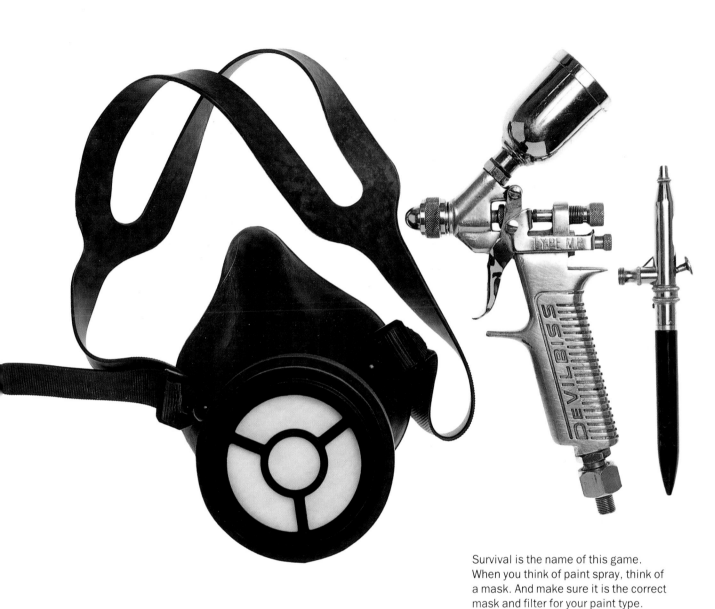

Survival is the name of this game.
When you think of paint spray, think of
a mask. And make sure it is the correct
mask and filter for your paint type.

The airbrush – a personal view

But the real nitty-gritty is the airbrush. That's where you really get
down to the business. I have had my old DeVilbiss Super 63A for 19
years. I get through machines very slowly!

Against the official instructions, I like to use it stripped down. The
black plastic handle is an encumbrance and upsets the balance of
the machine in your hand. It must be weightless, an extension of
your finger, a finger that shoots paint. You need instant access to
the needle also. But take care not to drop the instrument or 10 to 1
it will land on the back of the needle and drive it through the nozzle.
Very expensive and very nasty. Every time I change a colour I wash

Flight 704

the reservoir out, gently sliding the needle in and out. This makes sure there is absolutely no trace of the old colour left and helps keep the nozzle clear of blockages. But be gentle or you will damage the nozzle; the needle seats on it to close it and prevent any loss of paint.

To wash it, first dip the whole nose into a jar of water or whatever solvent you are using, up over the paint reservoir. Unscrew the clamping screw and withdraw the needle out past the reservoir, safely out of the way. Then brush all the old paint out into the jar. Now take the airbrush out of the water and spray the water left in the

This painting holds its illusion even on close inspection. Within the seemingly simple image there is great detail. The whole thing is based on very accurate measurement. The curve of the leading edge was achieved by drawing against a long rod under tension.

reservoir out through the nozzle, gently pulling the needle in and out. Seat the needle on to the nozzle and tighten the clamping screw and away you go again.

What if, when you are deep into a work, spraying with complete confidence, the paint stops? You look at the reservoir; it isn't empty, which means you have a blockage in the system – usually in the nozzle. You have got to get it out. My method will, again, make the manufacturers wince.

First I unscrew the nozzle cap and then I withdraw the nozzle, carefully, or the tiny rubber O-ring will fall out and completely disappear. No matter where you are it will disappear, believe me! Now I withdraw the needle and very gently work it into the back of the nozzle, easing the obstruction, usually some hardening paint, out through the nozzle front. I gently work the needle round until it is clear. If the obstruction is jammed into the very mouth of the nozzle, it's best not to push it forward but to withdraw the needle and with the utmost care insert the tip of the needle into the nozzle mouth, just enough to dislodge the obstruction. I complete this operation by blowing down the mouth. But you need A1 eyesight and a firm grip, or you'll do some more expensive damage.

When I'm sure all is clear, I replace everything and spray water through and start again. Of course, it's best not to get any blockage in the first place. But keeping paint granule-free is the last thing I think about when I'm deep into some recalcitrant image.

The really hard part is the finger control, the pressing and pulling on that tiny button. I can't tell you how to do that. It took me two years to learn, I mean really learn. And the wrist movement makes it more complicated. A gentle swaying movement is needed, like some hula dancer, that will allow the atomised paint to caress the canvas, leaving a soft, even colour. Build that colour up slowly, let each coat dry before you lay the next. Don't look at the machine, look at the picture. Practise if you're not sure. You will get so good eventually that you'll be able to draw a line with it.

Because the airbrush relies on a constant air pressure to maintain a constant flow of paint, it follows that an inconstant pressure will result in an inconstant flow of paint. In other words, you control the quality of spray by controlling the pressure. Very low pressure will result in a very speckled application to the canvas. Increase the pressure towards the recommended value and the speckling will decrease. You could buy a variable valve and slot it into the air line, or you can just put your heel on the line and squeeze the rubber. It works. It's also better to use a lower pressure if you want to do some intricate spraying.

If you're looking to get the speckled effect, or spattering on purpose, another way is to use the bigger DeVilbiss MP spray gun and run it on low pressure. Increase the pressure and the spatter gets finer until it becomes a spray. I used this for all my illusions of

The object is painted first, the background last. This is possible because of the effectiveness of the masking material. This procedure is purely to activate creative inspiration in my mind, it has no relation to any form of practical logic. Creation is not only dependent on the manipulation of tools and paint, but upon the manipulation of the mind.

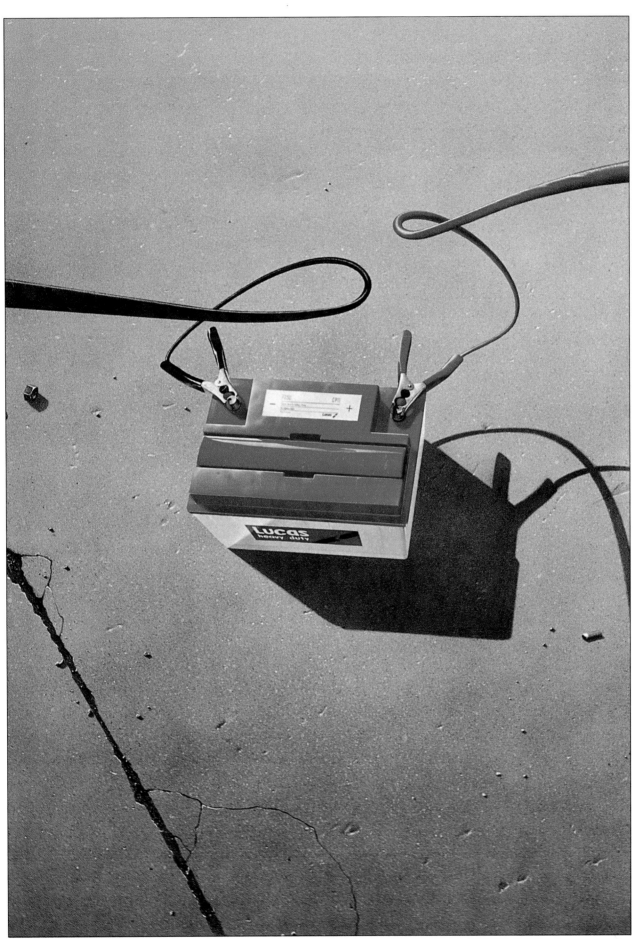

The Battery 1975

EQUIPMENT & APPLICATIONS

Sunlight and Steel 1986

The polished steel area is masked off before the circular spray work is started. Brushwork is combined with this system to achieve the irregularity of true realism. Note also the surface of the unpolished material.

rusted steel, mixed of course, with a bit of toothbrushing. You know, dip the brush in paint and flick it over the area you want to cover. The advantage of the toothbrush is that it doesn't give a constant even cover. And on rusted material the last thing I want is an even finish.

As for particular techniques, for instance I can draw a straight line by using the old signwriter's technique of the straight edge. You run a brush along a ruler held at an angle to the surface and brush a straight line. I can run an airbrush along a ruler, sitting the nozzle cap into the ruler edge, and airbrush a straight line. You need the lightest control on the button and you must sweep it quickly along the ruler's edge. If you are slow the line will flood and look horrible. With a good needle and nozzle set you can do wonders. With a worn needle and nozzle set it really becomes a struggle, because the paint won't come out evenly. And you must prevent any paint build-up in the nozzle cap or it will start to spatter. Keep it clean. If you do, after all that, get some spots on your painting, you can dab them off immediately with a tissue. Always have some tissue instantly available. And don't let the paint overflow from the reservoir on to the nozzle cap or you really will get spots. Keep checking.

There is a development of the airbrush-on-a-ruler system; instead of a straight line, you can make a circle. It's easy. I just tie some nylon fishing line to a nail and stick it in the centre of the proposed circle. The other end of the line I wind once round the airbrush at the required length and proceed to spray, moving the machine round the circle traced by the taut line. I hold the free length of line in my left hand taut as well. This enables me to slip the airbrush up and down the line to vary the diameter of the circle, or create other circles. But watch it. You need a steady hand. And remember that the circumference traced by the line will increase or decrease as you sweep the airbrush around the circle. You must compensate for this by paying in or out the line in your left hand. You can, of course, dispense with the left hand and just make a loop for the airbrush in the primary line. Then it won't wind in or out as you trace the circle. Not so easy after all, is it! But as can be seen in the *Fanjet* painting, it's very effective.

Sunlight and Steel (detail)

The ruling pen

Using the ruling pen has been another technique I have borrowed from the graphic designer. A lot safer than running a brush along a ruler, it gives me a clear strong line whose thickness can be pre-set. Ideal for radiator grilles, where each cooling fin has to be exactly the same width and density as the others. The ruling pen holds a good quantity of paint, so really long strokes are possible without the need to re-charge.

This is especially true when it is attached to a large-radius compass. My own extra-large system that I made myself consists merely of a 4-metre long steel rod upon which two lockable points slide. One is the centre point, the other is adapted to take either a pencil or a ruling pen. You can see the technique in all my wheel paintings. When it is allied to the circular airbrush system, the effect is very dramatic – shines and joints on metalwork are intensified and hardened.

I find however that too much reliance on the ruling pen makes for a very dull, uninspired image. Its asset – its consistency and reliability of line – works against it. The mechanically perfect strokes it makes do not exist in real life. Even precisely machined steel edges have a certain irregularity that only a fine brush can capture. Like all tools, it must be held in check and used only when absolutely necessary.

Masking

Masking is a whole world in itself, so I shall really lay down everything I know. Many of the realist artists like Don Eddy and Chuck Close don´t use a mask at all — or at least they don´t say they do. I rely on masking very heavily, though not all the time.

It´s interesting to see how my use of masking film was a follow-on from my involvement with the silk-screen process in the Sixties. The whole concept of silk screening is based on the mask; it adheres to the screen and the colour is squeezed through the unmasked areas. It´s the same process really — except now the mask is laid on to the support and the sprayed colour adheres to the unmasked areas. In the old days I was even pre-empting my latest airbrush work by using two or three colours in one print. We called it rainbowing. The inks would merge naturally to create a gradation of colour; in those old posters it was very effectively used as background, and the structure of the image was printed over later. When the artworks were presented to the printer, they were either in the form of a line drawing from which the printer hand-cut the screen mask, or a black-and-white artwork. The hand-cut work was generally for the large rainbowed areas and the black and white was photographical-ly transferred for the more complex structural parts of the image.

There are many different masking products available on the market nowadays, but in the late ´60´s the only stuff I could get was Frisket, an American adhesive film that Langford and Hill sold in Soho. It was a low-tack film, but not that low, so you had to be very careful when you peeled it off. Pull it off too quick and half the paper would come off with it.

When Frisket disappeared, a whole rash of new and better products appeared. The one I use now is made by the makers of Magic Marker, a bit hard to find. It is low tack, but not too low. It guarantees a sharp edge and won´t blow off the surface when you spray. There is nothing more irritating than finding the paint has sprayed or bled under the mask when you lift it off. That happens with the very low tack films. In fact if you use a high pressure gun the whole thing takes off out the window!

Masking film is excellent on smooth surfaces like card and smooth sythetic sheets, but on canvas it is hopeless unless the

The Move 1967

EQUIPMENT & APPLICATIONS

TBWA 1982

canvas has been so heavily primed that the weave disappears under the paint.

On canvas you need something stronger like clear adhesive tape, or adhesive covering film with a strong tack. Strangely, I find the cheaper quality tapes are better for this purpose; the more expensive types, including Sellotape, tend to expand and bubble when exposed to water, making a nonsense of your sharp line. But don't take this rule as gospel, because different standards apply in different countries. In many ways tape has the advantage over film as it can give you a ready-made straight line and an area can be covered with repeated strips.

The process of mask cutting is an art in itself, something not to be taken lightly. The precise control necessary to handle the knife will take as long to master as the airbrush itself. The secret is not to rush but to use a sharp knife – and for Christ's sake don't press too hard, or you will go through the canvas or make a score in the card that will ruin the final illusion. The pressure has got to be just enough to push the blade through the film or tape without making a mark on the painted surface. Not easy, especially as different masking materials need different pressures. With very simple cuts you can do the cutting before you place the film over the picture, and that way you get absolutely no mark at all. But make sure it's simple.

The film is so pliable that any complex cutting will twist and bend as you carry it over to the work. You try untangling a sheet that has stuck to itself – it's a nightmare, impossible in fact.

Low-tack mask film gives sharp, hard edges to images. So obviously, masks with no tack will give a soft edge. My favourite no-tack film is cellophane – the thinnest available is 2 thousandths of an inch, but often 3 thou. is a better bet, something a little stiffer to work with.

All I do is treat the cellophane like regular masking film and cut out the shapes. But where the tack film is firm on the work, the cellophane is free to move. So, I spray the area a very faint colour, move the cellophane, spray again, move it, spray again, move it and so on until I have the density of colour I want and the softness of edge I want. Another way is to lift the cellophane a little and let the

The title is scratched in the dust thrown
up on to the body. Note the masking
systems used on the labels.

colour bleed out. But I can never control the softness.

There is another way of masking, which I can't strictly call masking, but it was something I did in my really early work. This is cutting out previously coloured shapes, and it was usually to cover up a mistake. For instance, on the *Squeezy Tomato Dispenser* the ketchup running from the nozzle was first sprayed on cartridge paper, then cut to the form of the liquid on the painting, and then stuck down. The first attempt to paint the liquid failed so this is what I did. On the *Ball Strikes Water* all the little highlights on the water were cut from white paper. I am sure airbrush purists will hold their hands up in horror at this process; it isn't playing the game. But in my work every rule is to be broken. You wouldn't think so, by the formality of some of my paintings, but believe me, I am always on the lookout for new systems and new short-cuts.

Letraset masking

It has always been very difficult in realist painting to reproduce the fine lettering that appears on machines — instructions to do this, or not to do that, licensing labels or destination tickets. I guarantee that no one can paint a line of type and get it really correct. The line will always be a little wavy. The characters will be inconsistent in form and size. So what's the answer? Letraset.

Just draw out the line on the white canvas. Press black Letraset down in the form and type you want and spray it all over with the colour you need. Then when the paint has dried, pick the letters off with Sellotape. And you have a perfect line of white letters.

The system is easy when the background is darker than the letters. But when you reverse the procedure, for instance, red letters on white, then there is trouble as an awful lot of white is needed to cover the red and picking the Letraset up is not so easy. I circumnavigate the problem by only spraying a light coating of paint, picking the Letraset off and then thickening up the background with a small brush.

This system isn't compatible with oil-based paints so use only gouache or acrylic or ink. The molecules of oil-based products hold together too well and the Letraset cannot break the skin.

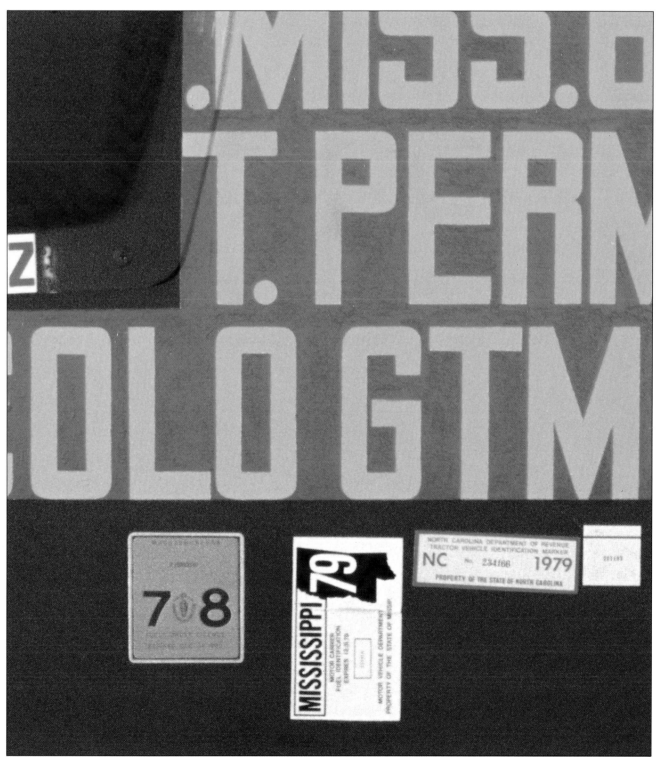

Letraset masking
Detail from *Wouldn't You Rather be Riding a Mule on Molok'ai?* See p113.

E Q U I P M E N T & A P P L I C A T I O N S

Blue Ford 1981

Here the machine was first painted, then white paint was thrown at the finished surface. The marks were then coloured red. This was one of my many attempts to break away from the limitations and confines of Hyper Realism — an attempt, I'm afraid, that demonstrably failed.

Yellow Diesel, Black Grease 1981

To achieve the tactility of the grease I laid black acrylic on to the image of the buffer with a palette knife. I then sprayed white paint along the surface from one direction, picking out the features in detail. A perfect example of paint spray imitating light. The effect was finished with a No.1 brush.

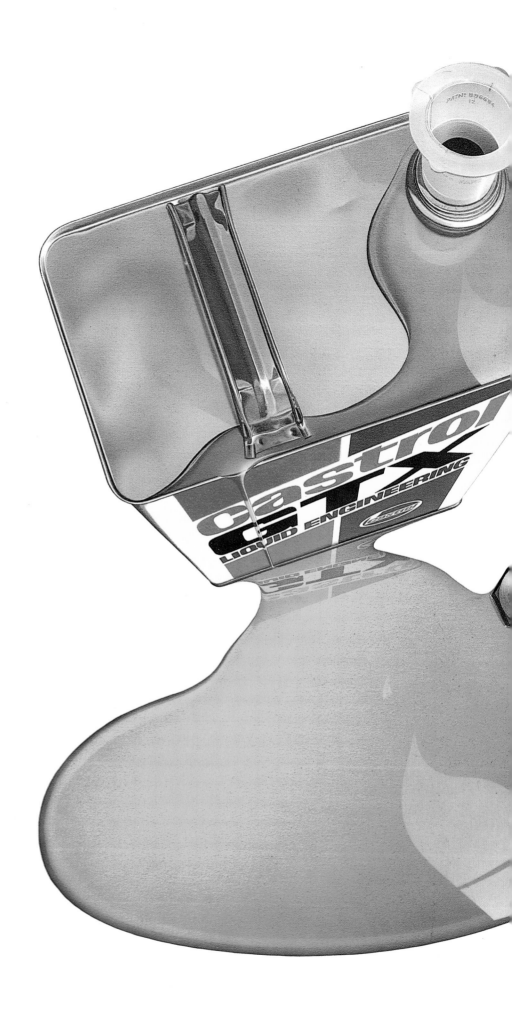

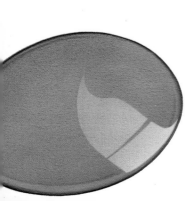

Castrol 1983

In spite of the difficulties and dangers of cutting complex shapes from masking film before laying it on to the image, I decided to take the risk and go ahead. It was extremely important to eliminate any traces of cutting on the canvas surface in the reflection area.

The reflection on top of the can was executed almost entirely with light strokes of Caran d'Ache pencil and not airbrush.

Paint

In the early days I imagined that Winsor and Newton Designer's Gouache was the only paint I could use. It was what I had always used in pre-airbrush days. Then I ran into Pelikan inks, which gave vibrant colours that sprayed easily, didn't clog the nozzle, and didn't have to be mixed up in a dish. But they were transparent. There was no room for mistakes. So I still carried on using gouache when I needed to. All my work up until the Machine paintings was a mixture of ink and gouache, though there is still a lot of ink and gouache in the steam locomotive picture, 75027.

Sometimes this is a rather dubious mixture but so far the pictures seem to have stood the test of time. (I have had no frantic calls from irate collectors yet!) Everything was fine as long as I never put gouache over ink. When a thick surface of Pelikan Ink dries, giving a deep colour, it becomes rather glossy. Laying gouache over this ink would be a disaster as it would have no key. In fact, keying is always something I watch for with spray painting; with a brush the paint is worked on, but spray settles and relies only on its own sticking power.

But you *can* put ink over gouache. The medium is partly absorbed by the gouache and the whole lot dries to a fairly solid mass. But it can be a bit powdery at times, especially with red. The surface can very easily be marked.

Once I realised that it was possible to spray any paint — I was even spraying my own car — it was inevitable that I should look for a more stable and practical medium. Oil was out. The fumes of sprayed diluted oil paint were unbearable. I'm sure I would be dead now if I had taken that route. No, I would have to go for acrylic. And, like most of my American contemporaries, that's what I have used exclusively since. It is easily thinned, it is water-soluble and it sprays very easily. It can get a bit lumpy, but as we have seen previously, that doesn't pose too much of a problem. Like oil, it is semi-transparent, but with a few layers, a real solid cover can be built up.

Liquitex Acrylic paint is what I always use now. I discovered it in the mid 1970's. It was only available in one or two shops in London then. It is an American paint made in Cincinnati, Ohio, really great stuff. Vibrant colour without being too acidic. It's still the best I have found. The pigments are all synthetic (you meet such frightening names as Phthalocyanine blue or Cadmium Barium Sulfide) but they still retain the warmth of natural pigments. But I will still use other paints with it sometimes. Many times in the past, if I wanted a really intense white I used Designer's Gouache permanent white again. And now I have even begun to use Caran d'Ache colours stroked over the sprayed colour. With care and patience I can get those intricate soft little areas as fine and delicate as any airbrush, but a lot smaller.

Brushes

I said before that the airbrush must never dominate the painting as it did in my early work. It must be held in check — disciplined, in fact. As I gained more control over the machine, so I restricted its use to area covering and light reflections. All the rest must be brush work. I have three brushes in constant use. Winsor & Newton series 3A, No.1, No.4 and a big flat one. But No.1 is the favourite. It has been the mainstay of all my work. With its long blade it holds a good quantity of paint and runs easily along a ruler — the old signwriter's technique of painting a straight line! It is small enough to allow me to work great detail into a picture but not too small to make the task of recharging too irritating.

The No.4 brush is used usually to cover larger areas, but together with the flat one I use it for dry brushing, another signwriter/ illustrator trick. If I dry-brush a white over a previously painted surface it gives the illusion of light, reflecting off a rough surface, perfect for some of the surfaces of heavy machines. I can do this with the airbrush too. Just by spraying white along the painting, instead of on to it, the same rough surface can be obtained. You have to hold the nozzle really low along the surface before you let fly, then wave it around along the same plane and the effect is magic and instant. A flat black surface becomes a road or a piece of a locomotive chassis. Just one stroke of the brush will activate my imagination. The secret of textural realism is the use of that white paint over the surface. The illusion holds no matter how close you are to the surface of the painting.

Ball Strikes Water 1971

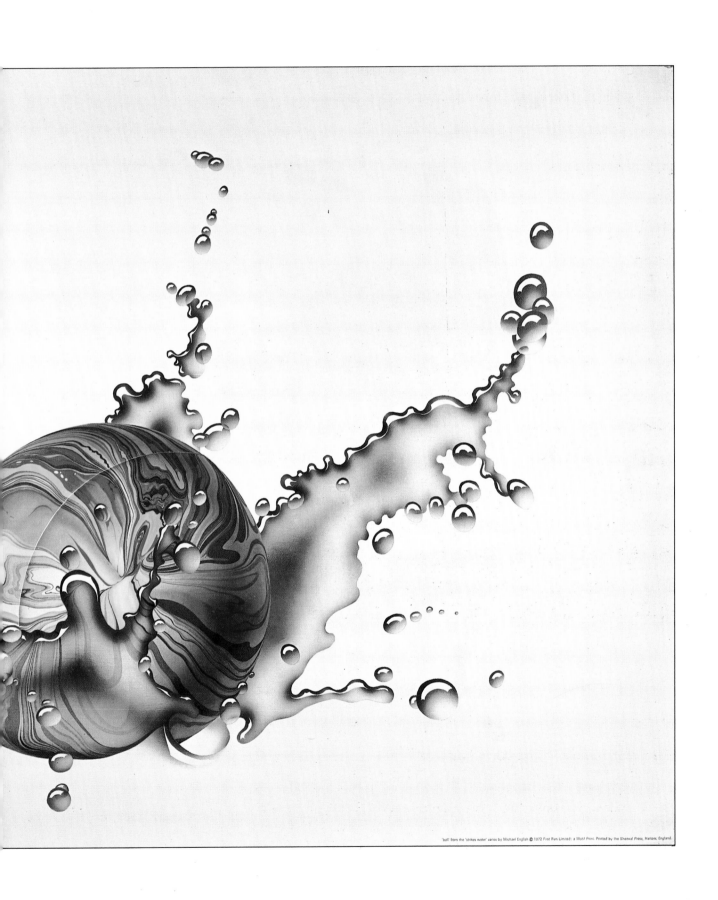

'ball' from the 'strikes water' series by Michael English © 1972 First Run Limited; a Mobil Print. Printed by the Sharwal Press, Harlow, England.

A Birthday Present for a Swiss Collector

Right: here the 'Letraset technique' is further complicated by distortion. This was achieved by 'doctoring' the letters after they had been laid down.

Evening Light, Paddington 1986

EQUIPMENT & APPLICATIONS

Fanjet 1977

The original drawings and photographs for this large work were made by standing on a servicing platform set up behind the aircraft, courtesy of Laker Airways. The outer casing was executed solely by the airbrush on a line and ruling pen on a rod.

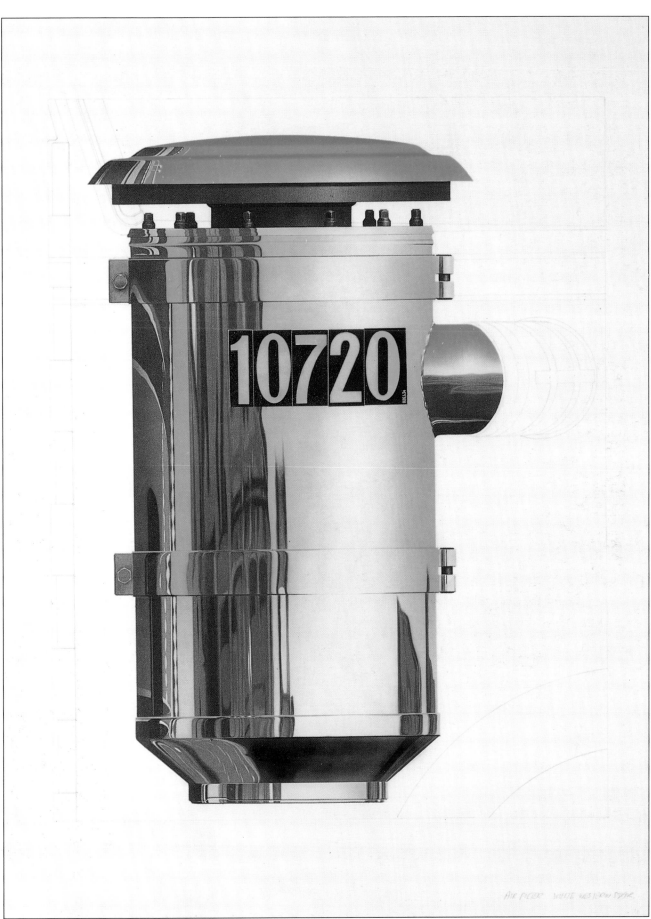

Air filter 1977
An unfinished study

California 1977
The United States is a stunning country for those oriented towards visual stimuli. Americans have a natural aptitude unmatched by any other nation in the world for creating visual delights. They do this quite unconsciously. This canvas was conceived as a homage to that magical gift.

Note the extremely complicated ruling pen work on the radiator and grille.

EQUIPMENT & APPLICATIONS

Views from the Schafferbergwand 1980

The inspiration for this triptych came from my walks high in the mountains. It's quite astonishing to see, close at hand, aircraft leaving vapour trails. Each picture is a view from a different altitude. This not only explains the proximity of the aircraft, but also the density of the blue.

E Q U I P M E N T   &   A P P L I C A T I O N S

An image that presented itself quite by accident in a California truck park. If you did not know that it was a container you would swear that the artist had at last escaped from realism. As in the other two pictures here, he is shown to be executing some sort of ballet between what he perceives outside himself and what is inside.

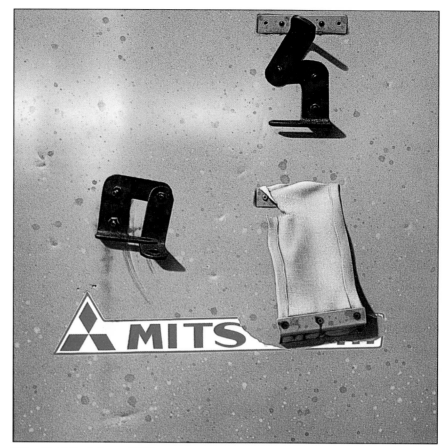

Mitsubishi Container 1986

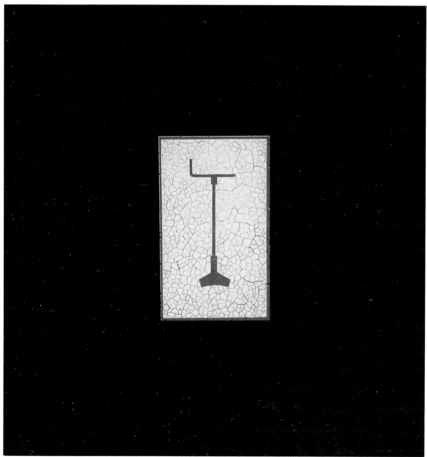

Regionalzug 1986

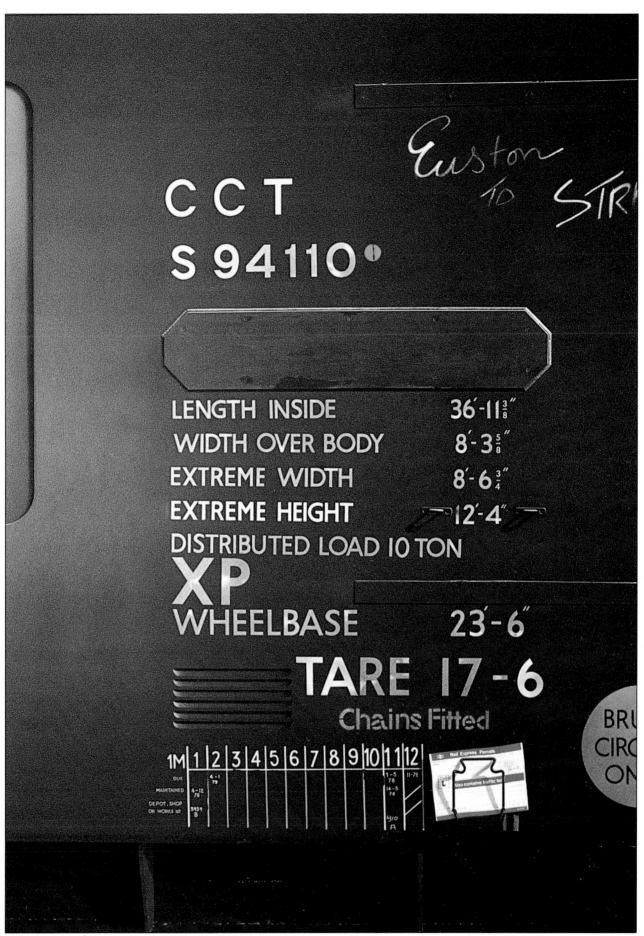

CCT
S 94110

Euston to STR

LENGTH INSIDE   36'-11⅜"
WIDTH OVER BODY   8'-3⅝"
EXTREME WIDTH   8'-6¾"
EXTREME HEIGHT   12'-4"
DISTRIBUTED LOAD 10 TON
XP
WHEELBASE   23'-6"

TARE 17-6
Chains Fitted

Man Machine 1978

Ferns 1974

An image of the secrecy of nature, from the time when I was less fascinated with machinery. Here the black background is laid on first with aerosol, then the vegetation and light points were painted in gouache.

CHAPTER THREE

TECHNIQUES & EFFECTS

Through all the years that I have worked I have always had, like most artists, a struggle to find techniques that will allow me to project the visions I have in my head on to the paper or canvas. I discovered pretty early in my life that, unless I mastered the medium I was working with, there was not much point in going on.

My type of representational art relies on the structure of the paint imitating the structure of the object. With this as a premise, I opened a whole new world of possibilities, but they could only work if I was free of the old traditions of painting. In a world of anything goes, anything can happen.

Oil on water

In the mid-Seventies I was always fascinated at the way oil or petrol created twisting, turning rainbows on water, in polluted streams or in gutters on the roadside.

All processes like this obey a certain law, one of the natural laws of fluid movement. This swirl effect applies whether it is paint on water, petrol on water, weather systems in the sky or galaxies in a universe. The movement pattern is the same. Sinuous, undulating, revolving. It is one of the most common patterns in nature. You see it flying over river estuaries. You see it in the way driving snow curls and twists over stone walls, and the way glittering clouds of fish turn and dance in sunlit water. It is there at the sides of country lanes after a rainstorm and in the eddies and currents of oceans. I tried every way to capture it, but it wasn't until I remembered that the process of painting must imitate the process and structure of the object that I finally broke the *impasse*.

Now I knew about the old marbling technique of pouring colour on to a liquid mixture of carrageen and water; the colour floats and can be moved about the surface and the resulting pattern is picked up by a treated paper.

So I developed my own system; filling the bath with water, sinking some previously dyed silk into it, and floating white oil paint — house oil paint — on to the surface. Then pulling it out so it imitates the shapes of oil on water, then drawing the silk up through it. The silk catches the paint and keeps it in its shape and relative position.

Oil on Water 1974

Raindrops 1989

It's a tricky business, but the result is fascinating. The silk is then dried, and the paint dries on it in the shape it was on the water. All that remains is to colour it and turn the whole abstract image into a stream. I would very gently airbrush the colour on to the white oil pattern. I was, however, unable to imitate the vivid iridescence of the real colours because paint, by its very nature, has no inner light. You cannot get a paint pigment to glow, as you cannot get white paint as bright as a light reflection – unless, of course, the background is dropped back into darkness, a technique exploited marvellously by Rembrandt. That way all the light colours really do glow and sparkle, but still not really as bright as the real thing.

Stone textures

I don't know why, but I just can't recreate random surfaces with either a paint brush or a pencil by direct working. I believe it's because the human brain (or is it just my brain?) creates images in its own particular form of progression, one mark growing and relating to the previous mark, until the whole surface is covered.

This *human* progression is not the same as the structural progression of a natural form or surface. The pattern we perceive is alien to us, because it was created by laws that are very different to the laws we make in our heads. Though we are of Nature ourselves, our creative processes have their own systems. I believe that it is

Right: after the surface had been treated and painted the focal image was painted on cartridge paper, cut out and laid into a similarly shaped slot cut into the 'rock'. This sophisticated method of collage is more akin to marquetry. It is worthwhile comparing this system with that on p53.

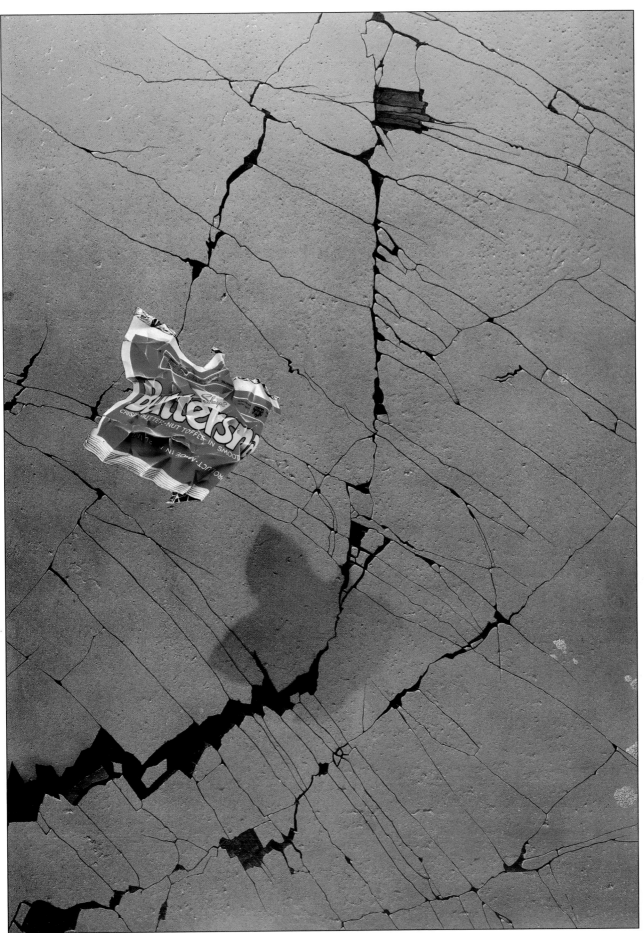

Rockface, North Devon 1975

precisely this difference, this alienness, this surprising freshness, that is the thing we call natural beauty.

So for another favourite of mine, the rock illusion, I had two techniques, both of which grew out of a desire to imitate the complex and random patterns of rock or concrete surfaces. I soon discovered that it would be impossible to laboriously brush-paint such a surface; the time taken would be completely prohibitive, let alone the difficulty of imitating a truly random pattern.

How was I going to get that natural textural structure of rock? The solution was obvious – imitate it. Steal the pattern and make it mine.

The first technique, straight imitation, involves buying a sheet of thick card and attacking its surface with a piece of rock or broken brick until the area I want for the surface illusion is well and truly indented. Then I spray a ground cover over the whole area, usually black or dark grey. Once this has dried, I apply the technique of spraying along the card with white paint – always in one direction, as light always comes from one direction.

Immediately the illusion of a rough surface comes alive. The paint picks out all the indentations and peaks in the rough surface.

I was very pleased, but not quite pleased enough. I needed to make it more real. So I developed the second idea, which was a little more than imitation.

I begin with a slice of white acid-free tissue paper. Then I look for a suitable piece of ground – a flat piece of rock, or a rough area of concrete (not too rough) – and lay the paper over the area. Then I take off my shoes and socks and gently press the paper with my bare feet into the surface form of the rock or concrete. The paper follows the surface exactly. This I take back into the studio and proceed to spray along the surface, dark grey or black one way and white the other. Now the form of the rock appears like a miracle. But if you try this, remember it's important to use a waterproof paint, for reasons we shall see a little later.

Once all this is thoroughly dry I gently iron the back of the paper flat, and am left with a sheet of tissue with the illusion of rock as though printed on it.

But now comes the really tricky bit. I paint the back with wallpaper glue and lay the whole sheet on to a piece of card. When

Illustration commissioned by Vogue magazine 1975

you wet tissue it becomes very, very fragile. One mistake and you have had it. And if you have a specific area on a painting you want to cover then it gets even more difficult. When lifting the wet tissue it's best to stick one edge along a ruler first. That way the sheet will remain a sheet. Lift it with your fingers and you will tear it apart. It is very, very fragile. I wish you the best of luck with that one!

My first attempts with this process weren't very successful, not because I could not create the illusion and stick it down, but because I couldn't make that illusion connect with the wider illusion of the painting. For instance, the painting *Reflection*, with what was supposed to be sky reflected in a puddle, failed because I couldn't see that a puddle has a damp edge to it. It is surrounded by damp rock. That painting has always irritated me. Why did I not see it at the time? It completely unbalanced the realism, so much that it became surrealism.

Sand and dust

Now there's another random natural pattern that the human brain cannot copy — sand or dust. But with an MP spray gun you can copy it. Not with a spatter cap on an airbrush. The spots are too even. No, the spray gun with very low pressure is perfect. I just lay a dark background then build up the grains until the effect is complete. For sand I use a yellowish white, for dust a very pale grey. Somehow the spray gun comes between the human hand and the picture. The low pressure air slowly pulls the paint from the well and randomly throws it on to the surface in little spots. That randomness exactly mirrors the randomness of the natural form. The lower the pressure the bigger the spots.

Something similar can be achieved with the toothbrush. Dip it in paint and flick the bristles. The paint spatters on to the surface in a really random manner. Big splashes, small spots, long streaks. I press some of the big spots with my hand, which spreads the paint out, making everything even more untidy. Just right for rust on steel. Lay the dark grey down, spatter it with rust colour, then when it's dry spray white along the surface. The result is real tactile cold cast steel. This is best done on canvas — It's like action painting under control.

Reflection 1974

This journey into texturalism has thrown up many other ideas and techniques. Some have remained just ideas, stillborn simply because there has been no practical or economic way of realising them. But there are two which must be mentioned, though I have rarely used them.

The first involves dabbing or rolling rough surface material, which has first been impregnated with white (or nearly white) paint, on to a previously sprayed surface. I have used everything from sponge to rag, to screwed-up tissue paper, to a house painter's paint roller. By dabbing or rolling very gently it is possible to turn a flat colour into a coarse rugged form that can, with imaginative brushwork, become something really three-dimensional. By overspraying this pale random pattern with a little of the previous colour you can really enhance the illusion. This system comes into its own with natural materials like tree bark, brick and stone, the flesh of fruit and coarse cement.

But you must remember that it is not enough to leave the pattern to its own devices, rather you must use it as a jumping-off point. Look at the patterns and imagine the ridges and gullies. Then use your paintbrush to draw forth these imaginings into tangible illusions.

This is really a message for all painting; I mean the use of marks of paint on canvas or paper to stimulate one's mind to throw up new sets of imagining, fresh ideas. Rather like the Rorschach effect of ink blotting. You can see how my realism has transcended representation and becomes more like abstraction, though retaining the cloak of realism. An interplay between what we see outside our eyes and what we see behind them.

The second idea is still just a party trick, an instant illusion that never fails to impress. Take a sheet of white paper and screw it up, then open it out and press it as flat as you can. Take the airbrush and spray dark grey along the plane of the paper from one direction, and white from the opposite direction. The creasing in the paper will be picked out in relief — it can look almost like silver paper. When everything is thoroughly dry, iron the sheet flat, and though the actual creases will disappear the illusion will remain. The result can then be gently over-sprayed with colour.

Shield 1986
A study in texture. The rough surface
was achieved by rolling thick acrylic
through a mask directly on to the card.
The numbering is dabbed with a
sponge through a hand-cut stencil. The
tape is bandage stuck directly on to the
surface.

TECHNIQUES & EFFECTS

Pack Fall 1980

A limited edition lithograph
commissioned by Philip Morris Inc. As
with many of my earlier lithographs,
the printing was allowed to run on into
an unsigned edition.

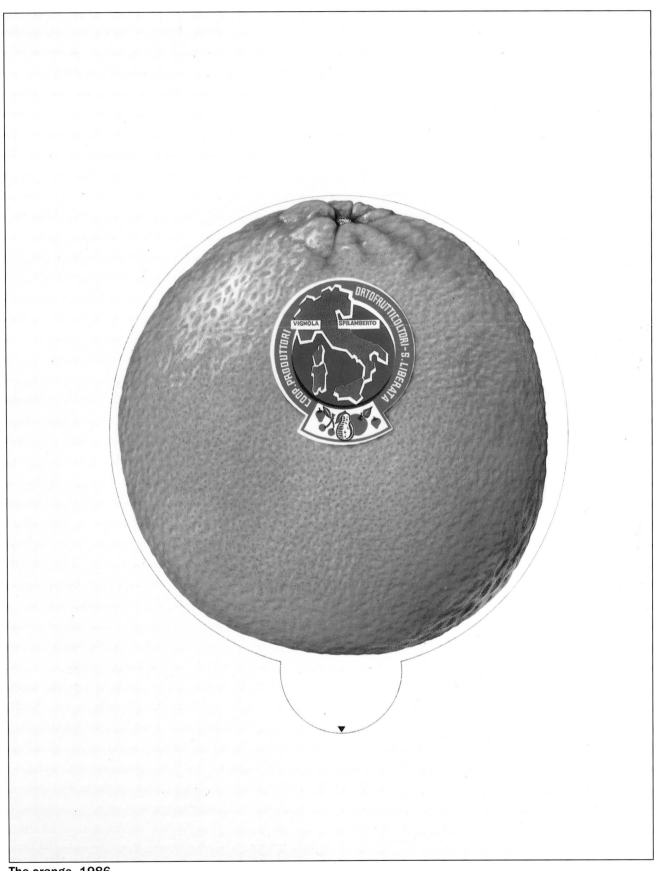

The orange 1986

The rock illusion technique does not necessarily need to be restricted to rock and concrete alone. The system can equally apply to any natural random surface pattern. Here for instance, the indented surface was achieved simply by striking the soft card with a round head hammer.

Silk screening

The tactility of paintings has always been close to my heart. The awareness of real as well as illusory form can be traced throughout my work. Even my earliest poster work was screen printed, an extremely tactile medium. I loved the way the solid metallic inks spread over the thin colour, forming a surface difference that could be felt.

My almost total dedication to the silk screen process in the later Sixties left its mark right through my machine paintings in the later Seventies. I learned from artists like Roy Lichtenstein and Andy Warhol that it was possible to print on to prepared canvas and still achieve a good crisp-edged image. I first used this system on a rather macabre painting of synthetic clothing – I thought here was a chance to make a good statement about stay-pressed clothes.

The repeat pattern is made with the silk screen, printed as you would if you were doing material or wallpaper. Then the form – or lack of it – is worked on top.

A much more exciting silk screen-assisted painting is the jet engine picture *Fanjet*. If you look closely at the inside of the main body shell you will see a pattern of perforations, part of the sound insulation system. It would be impossible to paint these and retain the mechanical regularity of the pattern. So I made a small piece of the pattern, photographically transferred it on to a screen and printed it down, marrying each area to the previous one, until the required area was covered. The result was very successful, I'm sure you'll agree.

It's important to use matt screen-printing ink rather than regular artist's paint, which doesn't have the correct consistency to give a good clean image. The screen ink is matt enough to accept normal paint, even water-based acrylic.

Synthetic 1975

Fanjet detail

The illusion of perforated steel is obtained by a repeat silk-screen printing. The ink bonds very well to acrylic paint.

Poster, 1987

Ikon 1987

This picture encapsulates, more than any other of my machine pieces, the contradictions within my own personality. The glorification of man's dominance of this planet, and the terror that this dominance can bring.

The polished black car does not reflect the dawn, but some distant industrial inferno whose sinister glow lights up the night sky. This painting is a warning for the future, an apocalypse that may just be avoided.

METHOD COMPOSITION & CANVASES

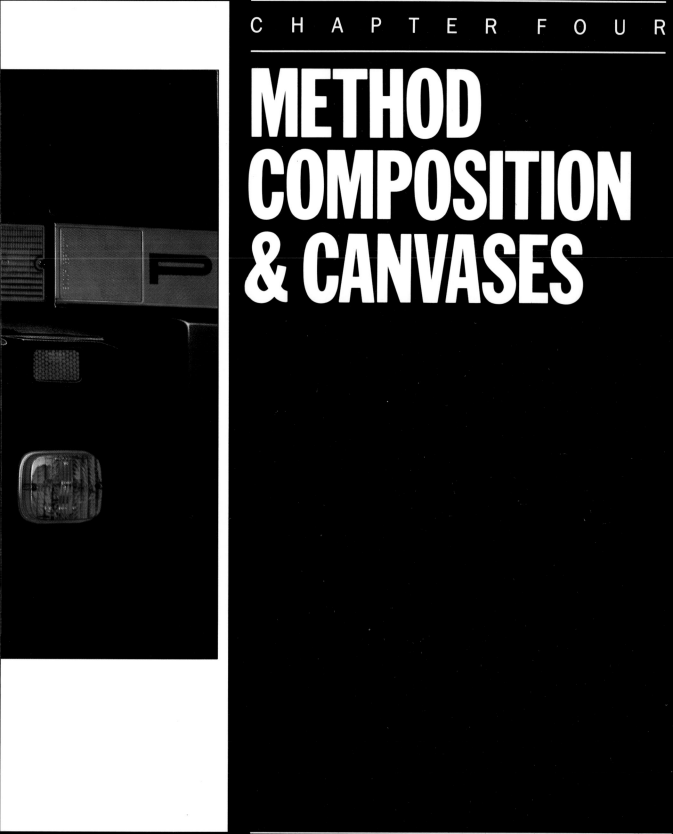

Perhaps the most fascinating of all techniques is the way an artist builds his picture. Each seems to have developed their own system. For instance did you know that Don Eddy, one of the American Photo Realists, actually constructs an image the way a printer constructs it? First he lays down the blue, then the yellow, then the red, then the black and white. That would be psychologically impossible for me, I just couldn't handle it. But it *is* a way of keeping the unity of composition.

Construction

No. My system is something different. I work as though painting by numbers. The whole composition is drawn up on to the canvas or card from a small line drawing which was taken from life. If the final painting is relatively small I generally use a Grant projector, an enlarging machine, where the small drawing is placed beneath a lens and the image is focussed up onto a glass table. A larger sheet of paper is placed over the glass and the enlarged image is traced off. It's rather like a camera obscura. This system was used exclusively for the 'Food' and 'Rubbish' series of prints.

When I have the enlarged tracing I turn the sheet over and trace the image again. Then the sheet is laid over the card or canvas and the image is rubbed down with a sharpened wood point. Take it away and there is your image drawn out on the picture, ready to paint.

Now a large painting requires a different and far more direct procedure. It's very simple really. Once I have completed a field drawing of the subject, a very accurate line drawing in fact, I build the canvas to the dimensions I want. These dimensions are scaled down on to the drawing to a given ratio. This is the ratio I now use to transfer the small image on to the large canvas. Using a calculator I merely multiply every measurement in the drawing by this ratio to give me the correct measurement on the painting.

Once the whole thing is complete I begin to paint, covering each area in turn — completing each area in turn, in fact, as though I'm building the painting with bricks. Each area or brick is an entity in itself, and it relates in my mind to the whole composition. I must always keep the final concept in mind, though of course, the final concept is likely to change as I see the way the painting is growing.

V-Neck 1975

As the 'bricks' grow, so they affect the original idea. My mind is always open to a new direction. At times I am likely to go back and repaint areas that were seemingly complete, because the final concept has changed. For instance, an area that seemed good when it was completed might look terrible when a following section is coloured in. I have learned how to paint a little better, so I must go back and bring everything else up to this new standard. Painting is a process of discovery, of mastering the technique. It's a process that can cause a lot of heartache, and a lot of joy. I find that once that heartache and joy has gone, then I have completely cracked all the problems of that style. My interest wanes and the work becomes increasingly monotonous and boring.

Canvases

I have always made my own frames and stretched my own canvas. I have to do everything myself! It's an uncontrollable compulsion. But really I just couldn't find any stretcher manufacturer who would supply me with what I needed. The frame must be solid and impart a certain form to the painting. It must be easily dismantled and reconstructed for transportation. When I took a 10×6ft painting to Switzerland in my car, the whole thing came to pieces and was packed away neatly. The canvas was rolled on a tube. The stretchers are made of 2×2in prepared softwood, cut at 45° and screwed together across the corners. A further cross-member of hardwood is rebated into the frame to give lateral support. The canvas is stretched and stapled to the frame then sized with Polycell wallpaper glue. I generally use Dulux Brilliant White Emulsion paint as the ground rather than the usual white gesso. The gesso gives too coarse a surface for the airbrush. The paint is diluted and applied with a small sponge and not a brush. I never paint the image right up to the edge. I like the idea of the white border. It seems to emphasise the impression of structural volume. These pictures are not only images but images on a tactile form. They stand out from the wall as though demanding attention.

One of my first real paintings, done in 1971, was the Grace Tomato Juice. This was a conventional Michael English image, but

Making frames

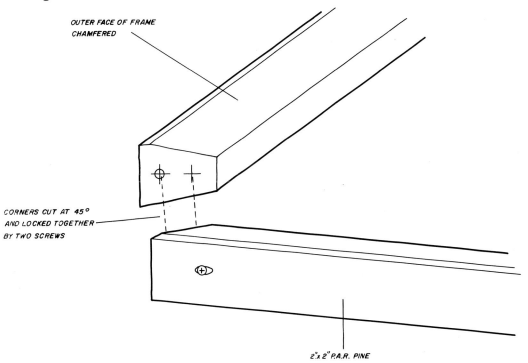

OUTER FACE OF FRAME
CHAMFERED

CORNERS CUT AT 45°
AND LOCKED TOGETHER
BY TWO SCREWS

2"x 2" P.A.R. PINE

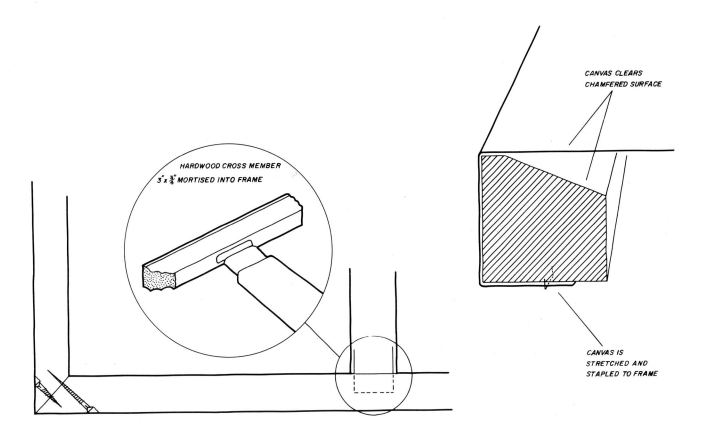

HARDWOOD CROSS MEMBER
3" x ¾" MORTISED INTO FRAME

CANVAS CLEARS
CHAMFERED SURFACE

CANVAS IS
STRETCHED AND
STAPLED TO FRAME

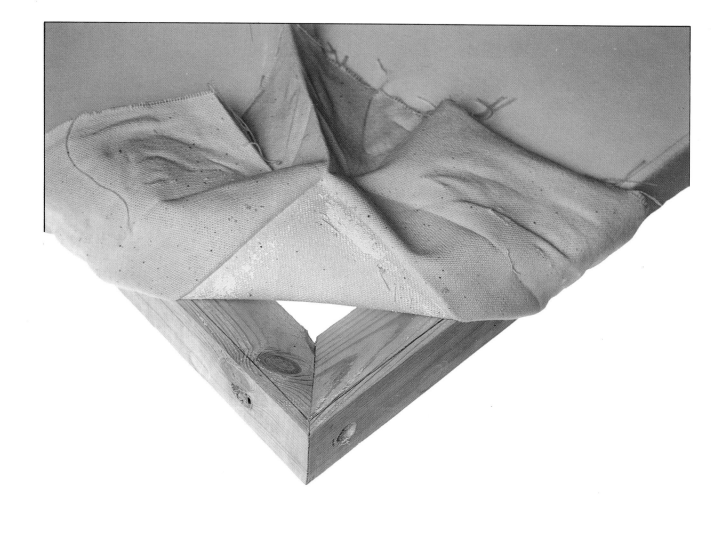

You can see here the completed
structure. The canvas is stretched and
stapled to the frame. Dismantling is
simple.

The Grille 1978

Metallic car paint sprayed on to sealed balsa wood. The joints between the shaped sections and flat surface are filled with car body filler, which is then sanded to blend smoothly into the shape I want.

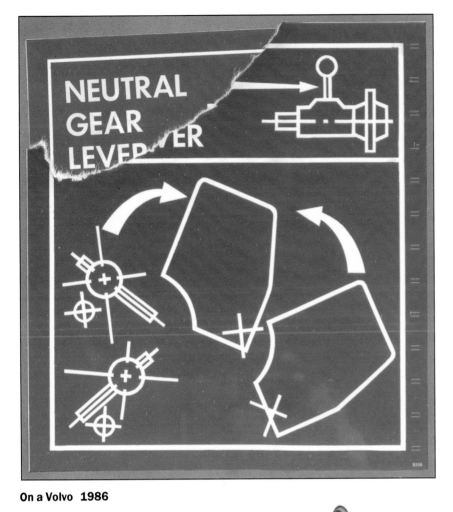

On a Volvo 1986

You can see here, very clearly, how a chance observation of some seemingly insignificant piece of information can provoke a surprise creative response. I can never relax for fear of passing that opportunity by.

A simple replica of a common traffic symbol. Cut from hardboard, masked and sprayed with cellulose paint, this little work has actually been used as a working sign, to create the damage patterns.

Long load 1986

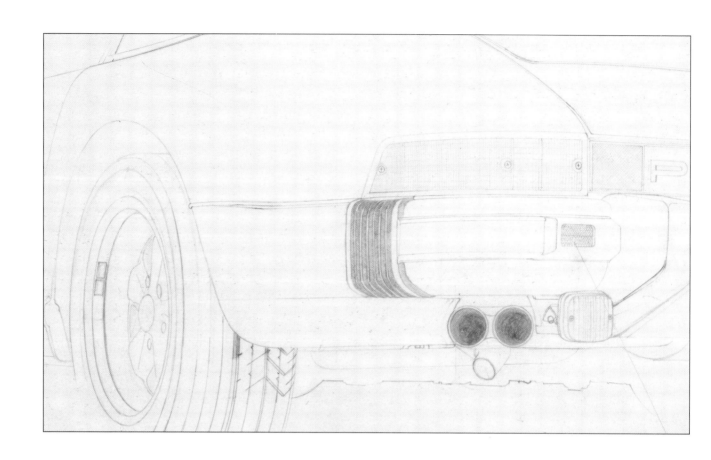

Ikon Progressives

Here again the construction imitates the real thing, each panel being assembled in strict order. I find that sheets from old telephone directories are ideal for masking – they are both easy to handle and dense enough to absorb the overspray. Once the black is laid down, it is worked over with airbrush and Caran d'Ache pencil.

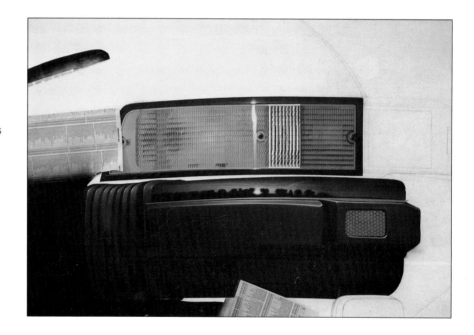

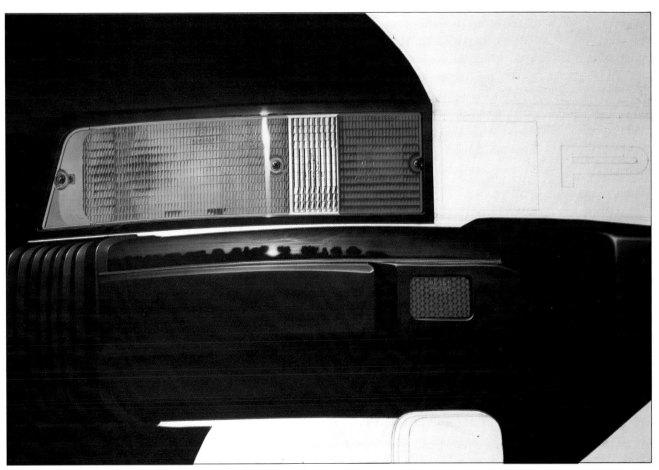

the catch was it was painted onto ½in blockboard and then cut out. It is in two pieces. The pouring liquid section slots into the can section.

More recently, and this was my first attempt to escape from Realism or Illusionism, I built two paintings, *Wouldn't You Rather be Riding a Mule on Molokai* and *The Grille*. Neither is representational of any particular subject, more an embodiment of a common idea. They were the result of two days walking around Manhattan. Very American images, both of them.

The stretcher and canvas are conventional but the structures on the pictures are made of balsa wood. Balsa is light and easy to work; when it is fixed to the stretched canvas the canvas will not sag. The balsa is cut and shaped like an architect's model, then sealed, sanded and sprayed. In these pictures the dominant feature is form and texture rather than illusion. But I felt that these two paintings didn't show a new way for me, so they remain just two of a kind. My interest lies in other areas now.

Silk

The Japanese use of silk for a painting support attracted me early on. It is a beautiful material, which when it is sized holds an image with great accuracy. When it's unsized, the colours run, which is a beauty in itself. My system was to stretch the material over a light wood frame, staple it round the back as I do a canvas and then sponge it with size. The surface is so delicate, like gossamer. It accepts gouache and water colour with ease. Whether painted or sprayed, the effect is very satisfactory.

Silk is something I haven't yet finished with – I've only scratched the surface of its potential. Its semi-transparent nature allows previously worked drawings to be directly traced through the material, which makes for less labour and a more direct relationship with the spontaneity of the original.

Unfinished

To show the progression of a 'nature series' painting. The undergrowth creeps across the surface of the canvas as though it were growing, slowly spreading across bare soil.

Grace Tomato Juice 1973
Gouache and ink on shaped
blockboard.

Wouldn't You Rather Be Riding a Mule on Molokai? 1987

Silk — Cashmere 1979

There is no airbrush here. The whole image was laboriously painted on to sized silk.

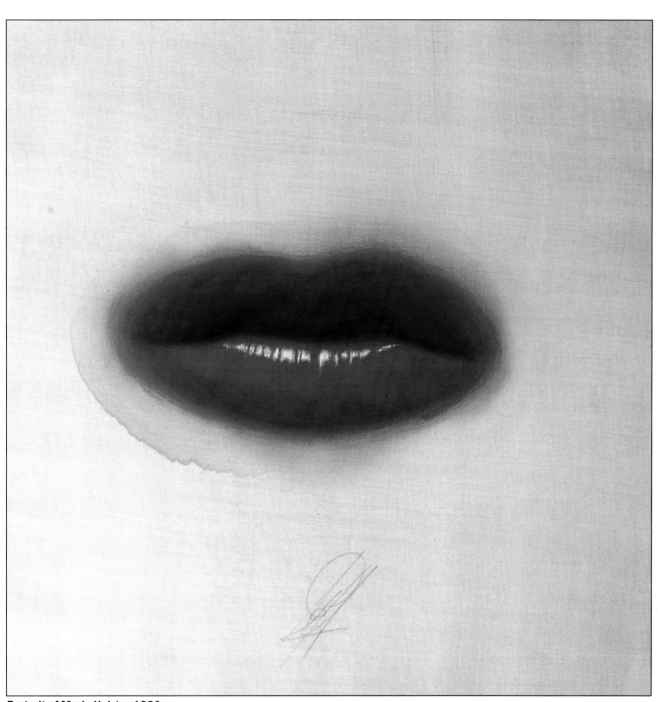

Portrait of Marie Helvin 1980

Here the silk was not sized. The colour was allowed to run freely on to the material.

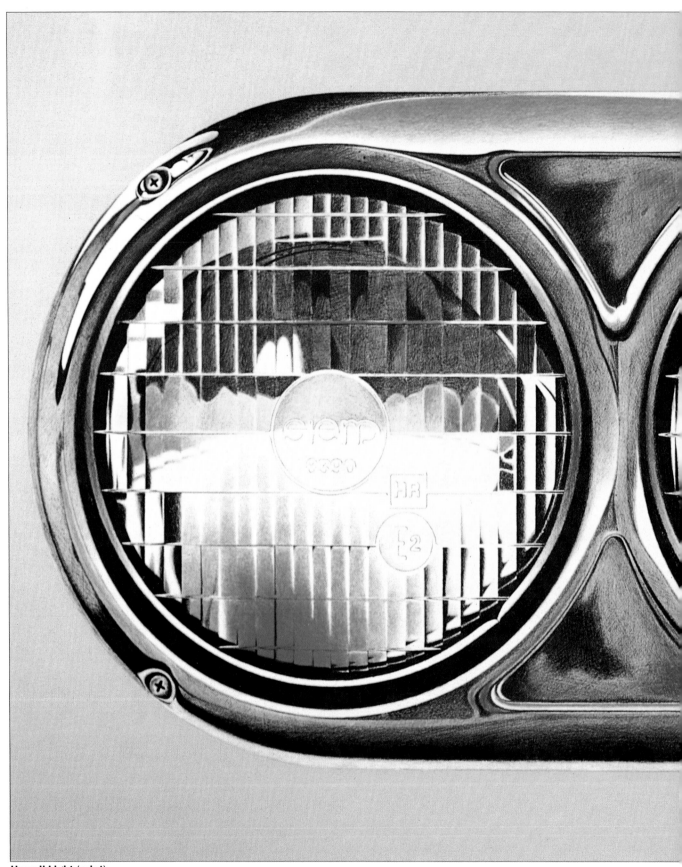

Hawaii Light (print)

This lithograph, my only attempt so far, was worked directly on to stone using litho crayon – no airbrush. The tones and colour were built up by using fine cross-hatching. Being used to the silk-screen process, I was disappointed at the dullness of the colour. But that's the nature of the medium – especially when printed on handmade paper. I shall have to do some re-thinking before making another attempt at this process.

Pick-up Truck 1986

I snapped and drew this truck in
Kaunakakai, the little tin-roofed
capital of Moloka'i. The truck was
originally blue. But in all my work, I
tend to alter true reality somewhat to
increase the effect of illusion.

CONCLUSION

So that has been the sum total of the first half of my life. I have set out all I can remember, and most of what I have learned, or at least, most of what I remember I have learned. There is probably much more but you will only find that in my paintings.

I chose the road of realism rather than abstraction because I felt that it gave voice to the feelings I have had about the tangible world around me. I wanted to make contact with objects, both natural and man-made, that existed outside my head. I felt that abstraction was the easy option, was introverted and selfish, man looking at his own navel. My paintings have never been paintings of despair. Some of the early ones seem a little shallow, even bad taste. But the better ones? Well, I am very proud of them. They succeed in radiating the joy I have had in living and experiencing the changing space around me. I feel so lucky to live in this dream called Life and to be able to come close, through pictures, to other lives outside myself.

In my twenties my ambition for success was a fuel that drove my paintings. And by success I mean fame. I see now how shallow that was. I see also that I never could become that superstar because I always wanted to get fame on my terms — alone. My personality is a solitary one. I am happiest solving my creative problems by myself and I find the human complexities of co-operation difficult.

This psychology is, of course, perfect for a painter, who must spend most of his or her working life alone in front of a canvas. But it doesn't help to win friends and influence people.

But what the hell. When it all comes down to it, what is it to be held in high esteem by the world? When my fragile life is over and I sink into the nothing that I came from, when I no longer exist and a million years flash by in a microsecond, all my regrets and failures, all my hopes and successes will be gone.

Painting is a way of cheating death. The pictures I leave will live well beyond my lifespan. If they are looked after they will live for a thousand years. I will not live more than ninety. Like all art they can speak across time. They transcend mere fashion and give messages of hope or despair, of joy or passion to all generations of our species. A great painting is at the apex of a triangle whose base is man changing. No matter where the observer is she or he can see the apex and can feel the same warmth.

Antipodean Honda   1986

Though small, this painting remains one of my favourites. I had so much pleasure painting, with great care, the random brush marks. The distorted and rusty chrome was somewhat altered from that of the subject, to heighten the compositional impact. Once again Caran d'Ache played a large part in the execution.

Because the human species, like all species, is a single organism whose body stretches not only through space, but also through time. Each member or cell of this organism lives to perform a particular role, then dies to be replaced by another. The death of any particular member is of no consequence, but the death of the whole is of the greatest importance. This is another reason why we can grasp the aesthetics of other ages. When we see a Renaissance painting we see it across time. We experience the whole organism. It is not alien. We have known it all along, deep within our unconscious. Works of art are the most valuable possessions we have because they spring from within the collective mind of the species. It is precisely this that makes them so magical.

Up until the early 1980s, realism was very much part of the mainstream of painting, and it was very good to have been part of that movement. But I remember being in the transit lounge of San Francisco Airport in 1983, picking up a newspaper and reading an account of a Julian Schnabel exhibition. The critic was appalled by what he had seen, calling it degrading and talentless, but I knew very well the writing was on the wall. A new generation of artists was rising up against us; and much to the delight of many other critics, we were overthrown. Pop realism was split asunder, and now the pieces lay scattered all over Europe and America, refugees in their own land.

At the beginning of this book I asserted that I had no desire for freedom of self-expression. Now, in this final chapter, I am not so sure. Perhaps, after all, an art so dominated by technique could never hope to last. In many ways, this hyper-realism was akin to post-impressionism. Both movements were influenced by the camera; the former by the precise accurate picture, the latter by the frosted-glass image plate. Both were concerned with depicting everyday life, the quotidian; both were destroyed by expressionism. Whether realism will ever be as sought-after and command such astronomical prices as Impressionism is another matter, one for conjecture.

In a world of over-exposure, no one was particularly outraged by the new hyper-real images. To a public fed on the excesses of modern advertising and TV journalism, it quickly became just

Wall Competition, Sperlonga, Italy 1986

another sugary taste to dull already overburdened senses.

Now there is nowhere to run, nowhere to hide save inside myself. I must free myself from the overpowering pressure of all the techniques that I have described in this book; return to the simplest materials and start again, up a different road. For it is the materials that dictate the nature of an image. The artist just follows along in amazement at the textures and colours that dazzle the eye.

So the last picture you see in this book is something very different. No airbrushing, no masking, no tricks. Just a very large sheet of cartridge paper stretched over board; just turning, twisting marks of pure graphite and an image of a tropical forest.

In the depths of a palm jungle the air is cooler. The hot equatorial sun can hardly penetrate the canopy of green. Only occasional shafts of light flicker across the trunks of the screw pines and play on the deep greens of the young Coca de Mer. Sunbirds flit in and out of the shadows. The only sound here is the beat of their tiny wings and the clash of the palm leaves in the wind.

This picture is the first tentative step away from the world of twentieth-century technology. A door that I am walking through. You cannot see what lies behind that door. But I can tell you that whatever it is, it is not airbrushed.

Vallée de Mai, Seychelles 1988
Graphite on paper

The author

AFTERWORD

There is a postscript to all this.

It is that I am still working. Trying to construct a new style; something that will encapsulate more completely the complex relationship I have with the world around me. So far my work has only scratched the surface — perhaps, after all, my realism has failed to satisfy me. Perhaps, after all, it is abstraction of some sort that can open up a new vision. I can only work and let the pictures carry me. I am in a darkened room full of people and I must find the lightswitch.

ACKNOWLEDGMENTS

The publishers wish to thank the following for their cooperation:
John and Gillian Aldington; Graham Bush; Urs Frey; Ford Jenkins;
Michael Pope; Roland Scotoni; Nigel Whiteley; Andrew Zulver.